THE ENTREPRENEURIAL ITCH
Don't Scratch Until You Read This Book

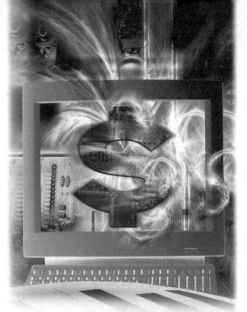

THE ENTREPRENEURIAL ITCH
Don't Scratch Until You Read This Book

David Trahair

Self-Counsel Press
(a division of)
International Self-Counsel Press Ltd.
USA   Canada

Self-Counsel Press acknowledges the financial support of the Government of Canada through the Book Publishing Industry Development Program (BPIDP) for our publishing activities.

Printed in Canada.

First edition: 2007

Library and Archives Canada Cataloguing in Publication

Trahair, David
    The entrepreneurial itch : don't scratch until you read this book / David Trahair.

(Self-counsel business series)
ISBN-13: 978-1-55180-735-5
ISBN-10: 1-55180-735-1

1. Small business. 2. Entrepreneurship. 3. New business enterprises. I. Title. II. Series.

HD62.5.T73 2006   658.1'14   C2006-905344-8

Acknowledgment

Figures 6 and 7, BillQuick Standard Report, copyright © 2005 are used by permission of BQE Software, Inc.

Self-Counsel Press Ltd.
(a division of)
International Self-Counsel Press Ltd.

1704 North State Street	1481 Charlotte Road
Bellingham, WA 98225	North Vancouver, BC V7J 1H1
USA	Canada

CONTENTS

1 WHY DO YOU WANT TO BE SELF-EMPLOYED? 1

You Hate Your Job 1

You Hate Aspects of Your Job 2

    The commute 2

    Annoying coworkers 2

    Making money for others 3

You Lose Your Job 3

Your Life Changes 4

Maybe You've Just Got the Urge 4

Why Listen to Me? 4

The Self-Employment Alternative 5

Do You Have the Entrepreneurial Itch? 7

How This Book Will Help Scratch Your Itch 7

2 WHAT DOES IT TAKE TO SUCCEED? 9

The Key to Success 9

Attributes of a Successful Entrepreneur 10

Attributes of a Successful Business 12

    Leg 1: Operations 12

    Leg 2: Selling and marketing 13

    Leg 3: Finance and administration 14

3 WHAT DO YOU WANT TO DO? 17

"A Restaurant Sounds Good" 18

Something Old? Something New? 19

Research, Research, Research 20

The Business Plan 23

Research Should Never End 25

Niche Today, Gone Tomorrow? 26

    What is good about a niche? 27

    Always be thinking about your next niche 27

4 IF YOU CAN SELL, YOU'LL DO WELL 31

What Doesn't Work 32

    The mailing list 32

    Expensive one-time advertising 33

    Newsletters 33

    Build a website and they will come 34

What Works (for Me) 35

    Personal contacts 35

    The story of my dentist 36

Other Keys to Marketing Your Business 37

5 GIVE YOURSELF A CHANCE: START ON A SHOESTRING 41

The Home Office 42

    Advantages of a home office 42

Disadvantages of a home office   42

Start-up Costs   43

Why Not Get the Bank to Help?   44

Where Does Cash Come From Besides a Bank Loan?   45

Your savings and "sweat equity"   45

Friends and family   45

Credit cards   46

The bank again   46

The Cash-Flow Crunch   47

Tips for easing the cash-flow crunch   47

Track your daily cash flow   49

6 BOOKKEEPING: LIFEBLOOD OF A BUSINESS   53

Basic Accounting Concepts   53

Accrual accounting   54

Debits and credits   55

Financial statements and journal entries   56

Equity   57

Capital assets, amortization, and depreciation   58

Bookkeeping for Sole Proprietors   59

Recording business finances separately makes
tax time easier   60

Recording business finances separately gives a
clearer view of your personal finances   60

Recording business finances separately lets you
see how your business is doing   61

Act Like a Corporation   61

Bookkeeping Made Easy   62

Invoicing and accounts receivable   62

Paying bills   63

Other bookkeeping entries   63

A word about using spreadsheets for bookkeeping   64

Setting Up Your Books 65

    Bookkeepers versus accountants 65

    The chart of accounts 66

    Schedule C — Profit or Loss from Business (US) 66

    Form T2124 — Statement of Business Activities (Canada) 67

    Group your expenses 68

Focus on the Key Numbers 71

Improving the Bottom Line 72

    Increasing revenue 72

    Cutting the right expenses 72

Keeping Current Is Key 74

7 AIM FOR THE IDEAL BUSINESS 75

The Ideal Client 75

    Pick and choose your clients 77

    Make sure your clients are in a solid industry 77

Get Others to Do the Work 78

    What kind of help do you need? 79

    When can you afford to hire someone? 79

Competing with You Is Difficult 80

Your Whole Family Is Not Tied Up in the Business 81

Could It Be Web-Based? 81

8 RUN YOUR BUSINESS; DON'T LET IT RUN YOU 83

Juggling Three Balls at Once 84

What's On Your Dashboard? 85

    My dashboard 86

    Other useful information 88

The Early Stage 88

The Growth Stage 89

9 IT'S NOT THE TIME, IT'S THE EFFORT   91

   The Good Old Hourly Rate   92

   Disadvantages of Hourly Billing   92

      It focuses on hours, not results   92

      It limits the amount of money you can make   93

      Billable hours become more important than
        business growth   94

      It treats customers unequally   94

      It doesn't reward the "finding" function   95

      It penalizes technological advances   95

   Hourly Billing Versus Set Fees   95

      Setting an hourly rate   96

      Going beyond time   97

      Value points   97

   Time-Tracking Secrets   98

      Keep track during the day   98

      Use increments of less than one hour   99

      Track chargeable and nonchargeable time   99

   Time-Tracking and Reporting Software   100

      What to look for   101

      The quest for five-star time-tracking and
        reporting software   101

      Why I chose BillQuick   103

10 INTEGRATE YOUR LIFE WITH YOUR BUSINESS   109

   Life Tip 1 — Do What You Don't Want to Do First   111

   Life Tip 2 — You Get What You Expect   111

   Life Tip 3 — Balance Is the Key   113

   Life Tip 4 — Plan on a Weekly, Not a Daily, Basis   113

   Life Tip 5 — Be Flexible with Your Time   114

   Life Tip 6 — Don't Be Afraid to Ask a Stupid Question   115

Life Tip 7 — Stay Away from Those Who Say You
Can't Do It   116

Life Tip 8 — Don't Be Afraid of Your Competition   117

Life Tip 9 — Leave Lots of Time for Completing
Each Task   118

Life Tip 10 — Don't Wait for Everything to Be Perfect   119

11 THE MILLIONAIRE DREAM: I'LL SELL IT AND GET RICH!   121

Business Valuation Methods   121

Business valuation method 1: Profit multiple   122

Business valuation method 2: Book value   124

Business valuation method 3: Service business   125

Are You Building It to Sell It?   126

Make it work without you   126

Make it big enough   127

Take time for planning   128

12 COULD A FRANCHISE BE FOR YOU?   131

What Is a Franchise Anyway?   131

Advantages of a franchise   132

Disadvantages of a franchise   133

How Much Is a Franchise Worth?   135

Questions to Ask Before You Buy   136

Watch Out for Scams   137

Examples of franchise fraud   138

How to spot a scam   139

The Five Most Frequently Asked Questions
about Franchises   140

Where can I get a company's presale disclosure
document?   140

How can I find out if there have been complaints
against a company?   141

How can I file a complaint against a company?   142

How do I know what must be included in a disclosure document or offering circular?   142

How can I find a lawyer who specializes in franchising?   143

13 THE SELF-EMPLOYMENT PENSION PLAN   145

Cushy Pension Plans Are Dying Out   145

Keeping a Job Is Getting Tougher   146

What Are You Going to Do?   146

Freedom 55?   147

I Love What I Do Now — Why Stop?   148

14 DO YOU STILL HAVE THE ENTREPRENEURIAL ITCH?   151

FIGURES

1   Cash versus accrual method of accounting   55

2   Sample journal entry: Income   56

3   Sample journal entry: Expense   57

4   Balance sheet   58

5   My dashboard   87

6   BillQuick work in progress report   105

7   BillQuick write up/write down report   106

8   Sale price based on a percentage of future billings   126

NOTICE TO READERS

1

WHY DO YOU WANT TO BE SELF-EMPLOYED?

Do you dream of saying good-bye to your boss forever? Do you wish for the flexibility of setting your own hours of work in order to enjoy more time with your kids or on your hobbies? Do you yearn to create a business of your very own? Do you imagine taking control of your life? If so, this book is for you.

There are many reasons why people might want to strike out on their own. Perhaps you simply don't like working for others. Maybe you even hate your job. Or you might love your job, but your company downsizes or your spouse moves to another city. Let's explore some of the most common reasons.

YOU HATE YOUR JOB

Two decades ago I was stuck in a job I hated, working for a boss I liked even less. Dragging myself out of bed each day was a chore. Sunday nights were torture. The thought of waking up the next morning and putting myself through another day of drudgery, criticism, and mindless effort was enough to keep my heart racing and my eyes wide open until the wee hours of the morning. I will never go back to that kind of life.

One thing that particularly drove me nuts was the implication that to be productive, I had to be in the office, sitting at my desk. It was important for the boss to see me coming in as much before 9:00 a.m. as possible and staying until 6:00 p.m. Skipping lunch? Good for you, Dave. It seemed this was more important than what I was actually producing. How useless was that?

I remember at the time feeling cornered. I couldn't quit — I needed the money. I started looking for another job, but that took time, which meant many more months of trying to satisfy a boss who never would be happy. It was a relief when I was finally able to leave and start my own business.

YOU HATE ASPECTS OF YOUR JOB

Maybe you like your job, but you hate the commute, or you dislike some of the people you work with, or you realize how much money your employer is making from your work. These reasons may be enough to motivate you to set up your own business.

The commute

I have met more than a few people who commute an hour and a half each way to the office — and that's when there is no traffic jam! That's a full three hours a day, 15 hours a week, or about 750 hours a year that they could be enjoying with their family or in a leisure activity. In other words, they have a full-time job five days a week for which they get paid, and they have a part-time job approximately two days a week for which they receive no compensation. Obviously some people don't have a choice — they need the job and don't have any other options — but it's going to take years out of your life.

Annoying coworkers

Perhaps you don't like the people you work with. Maybe some of your coworkers would stab you in the back in a second to get ahead. Or you may be forced to work with people who don't want to do any actual tasks, but who are great at taking credit for the finished project. You may have colleagues who are in the office before you arrive and stay longer than you every day, forcing you to work longer hours to show your commitment. Perhaps other colleagues are naturally miserable and think you should be too. Any of these irritants may encourage you to look for the exit.

Making money for others

There are many situations where people are working in a job and making a lot of money — for other people. Take a lawyer, for example. Law firms focus on one key thing: chargeable time. It's not uncommon for these firms to expect their employees and associates to put in 2,000 or more chargeable hours per year.

Let's translate that into days and weeks. Ignoring overtime for a moment, let's say Lindsay Lawyer works from 9:00 a.m. to 5:00 p.m., with an hour for lunch, five days a week. That's a 35-hour week. She takes two weeks off per year, so she puts in 50 weeks each year. That's 1,750 hours. To get to 2,000 hours, she has to put in another 250 hours of work. That's what overtime is for. She'll need to put in another seven full weeks of work to meet her target.

Lindsay makes pretty good money for her efforts: $125,000 a year. But wait just a minute — Lindsay's billing rate is $250 per hour. That means her firm is billing clients a total of $500,000 (2,000 hours at $250 per hour) for her services. Hmmm. The firm bills half a million and pays her $125,000. The firm's profit from Lindsay's work is $375,000. Hey, I feel like starting a law firm!

But what about poor Lindsay? She faces pressure every day to keep her chargeable hours up and keep clients happy at the same time. Something's got to give.

YOU LOSE YOUR JOB

You may be good at your job, but there is a real risk you could be shown the door. Step on the wrong toes once too often and you could be led to the boardroom to meet with a stranger who will help you try and find a new job. An even bigger danger today is that, in response to mergers and acquisitions and pressure to boost the bottom line, more and more companies are laying off masses of people without a second thought. Through no fault of your own, you could be given the boot. "Don't take it personally — we're just 'right-sizing'" is a common refrain. Face it, there is no such thing as job security anymore.

YOUR LIFE CHANGES

Perhaps there has been a change in your personal life that opens the door to starting your own business. For example, you've just had a baby and decided to become a stay-at-home mom or dad, but you don't want to lose all touch with the world of paid work. Or, a few years later, your little angel has just started daycare, so you finally have some free time. Or maybe your spouse has had to move to a new city where jobs in your field aren't plentiful. This is your chance to strike out on your own. Any of these changes may be the boost you need to unleash your inner desire to venture out on your own.

MAYBE YOU'VE JUST GOT THE URGE

Maybe there are no outside forces pushing you to start your own business. You actually like your job but would love to try something on your own. You love your hobby and want to turn it into a moneymaker. Or you have great plans to build an empire you and your descendants can be proud of.

It doesn't matter what the reason is, you've come to the right source — someone who had an urge just like yours, who has gone through it already.

WHY LISTEN TO ME?

Why should you listen to me? Well, first of all, I am 48 years old and have been self-employed for nearly two decades. I am not some hotshot kid, fresh from school, with ideas about what being self-employed is like. I have lived it.

I have struggled through growing my own business from scratch. I did not buy a business from someone else.

My business happens to be a service business. It started out as an accounting practice and has expanded into a financial services business. The advantage to this type of work is that I get to see hundreds of other businesses come and go — as clients. Some of them have been successful, and others are no longer in existence. This experience has allowed me to learn in two ways:

- The hard way — by making my own mistakes

- The easy way — by learning from other people's mistakes

THE SELF-EMPLOYMENT ALTERNATIVE

I am not going to say that being your own boss is perfect — it most definitely is not — but there are more than a few reasons why I love it:

- *Flexibility and variety.* You are in control — you can decide what type of business you want to get into, how many hours you'll work, and when you'll put in those hours. The time before you start your business is a key point in your life because you have the power to decide what you would like to spend the rest of your working days doing. It doesn't necessarily have to be what you are doing now. There are many success stories involving people who started businesses totally unrelated to the work they had been doing to that point: an engineer who started a lawn-and-garden maintenance business, for example, or an executive who opened a hair-salon franchise, a lawyer who set up a daycare business, or an insurance agent who established a bed-and-breakfast.

  Even if you like what you currently do for a living, being self-employed in the same field can free you from the shackles of reporting to a boss. There is no one telling you that you will write a report on subject A and that the conclusion should be X. That's probably what I like best — the variety of work and the fact that I can come to my own unbiased conclusions.

  You are also free to change the focus of your business along the way. For example, I started off in my business as an accountant, but I do much less accounting work than I used to because I find writing and speaking on small business and other financial matters more rewarding.

- *Work less, make more.* Okay, I admit I like this as much as the flexibility. Let's look at Lindsay Lawyer's case as an example. If she were self-employed and billed less than the $250 per hour she does now, say $195 per hour, she'd only have to work 641 hours to bill what she is earning now — $125,000.

    Of course, if she were self-employed, she'd have costs associated with running her own practice. She'd need a computer, software, office supplies, and an office, among other things. Let's say she works out of her home and keeps her first-year costs to $30,000. She'd need to bill clients $155,000 to be left with $125,000 profit. How many hours would she have to bill at her hourly rate of $195? Only 795. So she'd be able to work 1,205 hours less than the 2,000 she is now doing to earn her current salary. That's an amazing 60 percent reduction in the hours she'd need to put in.

    That's oversimplifying things a bit — she'd need to find clients first, for one thing — but I think you get the idea. (By the way, we'll look at how to attract clients in Chapter 4.)

- *Time off.* When you are self-employed, you have a large degree of control over when you work. If you are a consultant and do your best work late at night, you can take the mornings off. If your five-year-old is performing in a play on Friday afternoon, you can take the time off and finish your work on the weekend.

    This is especially important for me. My wife and I have a nine-year-old daughter, Cassidy, and a 13-year-old son, Kyle. It's important for me to spend time with my kids before they are too old to want their old man around.

    I have many special memories of seeing my kids grow up. When Kyle was in second grade, he went with his class on his first ski trip, and I was able to accompany them. Kyle was just learning to ski and had problems negotiating a T-bar (who didn't at first?). I'll never forget the sight of his gym teacher, Mr. Thompson, running up the hill by his side to make sure he got to the top safely. How do you put a price tag on that memory? You can't. Sometimes the benefits of self-employment can't be measured.

DO YOU HAVE THE ENTREPRENEURIAL ITCH?

I define the entrepreneurial itch as that basic urge to start your own business and be your own boss. Most people have the "itch" to some degree. Those who feel it the most are probably thinking seriously about venturing out on their own already. The fact that you have purchased this book puts you in this category.

The person with an average itch may have thought of the possibility of operating his or her own business, but for various reasons (i.e., financial pressures, fear of failure, etc.) will probably never pursue it. Those with a low-level itch do not spend much time thinking about being an entrepreneur.

If you have a strong itch, do yourself a favor: start spending time on it. The sad truth is that many people never get around to scratching their itch … until it's too late.

HOW THIS BOOK WILL HELP SCRATCH YOUR ITCH

This is not a how-to guide. It won't detail the regulatory and tax rules for starting and running a business. There are already many books available that fill this need. (Self-Counsel Press offers two of them: *Starting a Successful Business in America*, by Dale Davis and *Starting a Successful Business in Canada*, by Jack D. James.)

This is also not a book full of theory, written by someone who has studied self-employment but has never actually been self-employed. As far as I'm concerned, those theories are for textbooks, and a lot of them are wrong. What sounds good on paper often doesn't work in real life.

Instead, this book tells a story about what starting and running a small business is really like, warts and all.

I hope that by the end of this book you will be inspired to venture out on your own, armed with the knowledge you'll need to make your business a success. I want to do all that I can to protect the entrepreneurial flame that is burning in your heart right now.

I want you to protect that flame so it doesn't get blown out by bosses and other negative people who don't see your vision or your value. In short, I want to help you succeed on your own terms and in the long run. I want to get you out of where you are now and into a lifestyle that is flexible and rewarding, much like your dream at this very moment.

2

WHAT DOES IT TAKE TO SUCCEED?

Before you invest a lot of time, effort, and money in starting your own small business, you'd be wise to think about whether you have the ability to be an entrepreneur. There are certain attributes shared by successful entrepreneurs, and you should consider whether or not you have them (or can develop them) so you can gauge how well you might fit into this world.

THE KEY TO SUCCESS

I have no doubt that the key to success for a small business is the quality of the person running it. Even if you have a great product or service with a good marketing strategy, if you don't have the motivation, drive, and skills required to run the business, it is likely to fail.

The honest truth is that some people are not cut out to be entrepreneurs. Those people can avoid a lot of wasted effort, heartache, and expense by doing an honest self-evaluation early on. Don't fool yourself — if self-employment is not for you, the best time to realize it is now, before you begin.

ATTRIBUTES OF A SUCCESSFUL ENTREPRENEUR

You can learn many of the skills necessary to be a successful entrepreneur — for example, if you don't understand bookkeeping and financial statements, you can learn from books or courses (in fact, I devote Chapter 6 to this subject). The same can be said for other areas such as selling and marketing techniques (discussed in Chapter 4).

There are, however, certain innate qualities that are ingrained in the personalities or present in the lifestyles of successful small-business owners. Before leaping into the world of self-employment, you should conduct an analysis of your own personality, skills, and lifestyle to see if you are likely to succeed on your own.

Let's look at some of the main qualities that successful entrepreneurs tend to possess. You don't have to have them all, but your chances of success increase every time you say "That sounds like me" to the following descriptions:

- *Successful entrepreneurs love what they do.* Because they are doing work they enjoy, it doesn't seem like a job or a chore to them. This is what keeps them going during the tough times, when they have to work late nights and meet tight deadlines.

- *They are not daunted by hard work.* It is not easy to research, start, and run a small business. Making the dream a reality takes a lot of time and effort. Entrepreneurs are not afraid to work hard.

- *They are inquisitive and interested.* They are always reading and talking to other people about their interests and experiences, and they like to keep up with current trends and events. This is how they increase their personal contacts and discover "what's next" for their businesses.

- *They like to deal with people.* It doesn't matter whether the business produces goods or services, entrepreneurs need to deal with a broad range of people on a daily basis — from customers to suppliers to business partners and employees. They need to enjoy dealing with people to make things run smoothly.

- *They thrive in unstructured situations.* They generally don't like to be told what to do, when to do it, and how to do it. They enjoy the challenge of making all the decisions themselves.

- *They have good communication skills.* Whether it's writing business proposals, talking to a bank manager about a loan, or convincing a potential customer that their product is superior, they are able to get the point across effectively.

- *They have a supportive family.* They have the support of their family and do not ignore the importance of their lives outside the business.

- *They can cope with a fluctuating income.* These people realize there may be some years when their income is low. They plan ahead for these times so they don't put the whole business at risk — and they are confident things will get better.

- *They have (or can develop) necessary skills and experience.* They are not afraid to face their limitations, and they are prepared to acquire the skills they don't have or to hire people who already have them.

- *They recognize the value of good health.* Long hours and stressful situations take a lot out of you. These people realize the importance of regular exercise and a healthy diet.

Now that you have thought seriously about your own personal attributes, you have likely discovered you are not perfect. But if you are resolved to work on your weaker areas, you will improve your chances of success as an entrepreneur. The next thing to consider is the attributes your business will require to succeed.

ATTRIBUTES OF A SUCCESSFUL BUSINESS

Throughout my years of self-employment, I have seen hundreds of businesses come and go. This has given me an interesting perspective on what basic elements a business needs to succeed. I have concluded that a successful business is like a stool with three legs to keep it stable. They are —

- operations,

- selling and marketing, and

- finance and administration.

In order for a business to succeed in the long run, it needs to be actively engaged in all three functions. Let's look at each and see why.

Leg 1: Operations

The operations section of a business is the actual work that the business does. For a plumber it's fixing people's sinks and tubs. For computer consultants it's programming clients' computers or providing technical services. For bookkeepers it's keeping the books for clients' businesses. It's obviously vital that you be able to perform the work of the business. At least, it's vital until your business grows enough to be able to pay someone else to do the work for you.

Operations is where most people have the least amount of trouble. Unless you decide to start a business that you know nothing about — which is a risky strategy — you probably have the skills you need to do the work of your business.

In Chapter 4, when I talk about how to sell yourself and your business to clients, you'll see that it's essential that you be good at what you do. If you are good, word will spread to other customers. If you aren't, it won't. In fact, if you don't provide good services or sell good products to people, bad word-of-mouth will spread, and that will almost certainly kill your business before it begins to walk.

Most people who start a business know already how to do the work of the business — the operations part. They have one leg of the stool. Note that two types of businesses have a major advantage over all others because their operations involve one or the other leg of the stool:

- Bookkeepers and accountants generally have no trouble with finance and administration.

- Advertising executives and consultants usually have sales and marketing skills.

If you are thinking about starting one of these types of businesses, you already possess two-thirds of the skills you'll need to succeed. If your business is in any other field, you've got more work to do.

Leg 2: Selling and marketing

The second leg of the stool is selling and marketing. This is definitely my weak point. I was never taught how to sell or market anything in my life. I think this is one of the greatest flaws in the North American educational system today. No matter what we do, we need to be able to sell to be successful. Why aren't we taught how?

Everything I know about selling I learned one of three ways:

- By making mistakes myself

- By learning from clients who know how to sell

- By listening to, and reading books by, people who know how to sell

I discuss selling and marketing in Chapter 4, so I won't get into the details here, but think about it for a moment. You may be great at what you do. You may even be the best in your area. But how are you going to be successful, or even survive, if no one knows you exist?

The simple truth is that you need to think about what sales skills you have. If you don't have these skills, are you willing to work on them? If you are shy, are you willing to venture out and take some classes or attend networking training, such as Toastmasters? If the thought of selling scares you to death, you'll need to consider how you will get over this huge obstacle. If you are motivated, you can surmount it to some degree by reading books written by people who know how to sell. However, if you truly believe you will never become proficient at selling, you may have to find an associate you can work with who does know how to sell.

Leg 3: Finance and administration

This area is a strong suit for me, as you might expect. It's easy for me to keep accurate books, make sure bills and taxes are paid correctly, and file annual income tax returns as required. What about you?

I can't stress the importance of finance and administration enough. I'll even spend all of Chapter 6 talking about how to keep financial records.

Sadly, I have watched many businesses fail. One of the traits they shared was lousy financial records. They had receivables so old there was no chance they would ever collect any money. They owed back taxes and had been assessed late-filing penalties and interest charges by the government. They had received many "demand for payment" letters from suppliers and, in many cases, nasty letters from their banker asking when the line of credit was going to come down.

The people running these businesses saw their dream of self-employment turn into a nightmare. Not only did their business fail, but they were often left in deep personal debt or bankruptcy as a result.

Do yourself a favor: work on your bookkeeping and financial skills before attempting to start your own business. (I won't get into this in too much detail in this book, but Self-Counsel Press has several great books on the subject by Angie Mohr, including *Bookkeepers' Boot Camp* and *Financial Management 101.*) Alternatively, find a partner who has these skills, or accept the fact that you'll have to pay for a bookkeeper and perhaps an accountant as well.

I'll give it to you straight:

If you don't focus on the financial and administrative aspects of your business from Day One, you're pretty well doomed to fail from the start.

▣　　▣　　▣

Your next decision is a big one. Keeping in mind the attributes you need to be a successful entrepreneur and the three fundamental things that will keep a company stable, what business are you going to start?

• •

Learning from an expert: Benjamin Franklin

Benjamin Franklin was one of the most incredible people of all time. He was many things: an inventor, a philosopher, a scientist, a statesman, a musician, and an economist. He was also a small-business owner. In fact, he was one of the most amazing entrepreneurs of his day. His business, a printing shop, did so well that he was able to retire by early middle age to pursue his writing and other activities.

But why was he so successful? Let's look at his attributes.

First of all, he was interested in the people around him and always strove to make improvements to their lives. This natural curiosity drove him to invent many products — the cast-iron Franklin stove so people could warm their houses with less wood, the lightning rod to protect buildings and ships from lightning damage, bifocals so people could see both near and far with the same glasses, and a simple odometer so he could figure out the shortest routes for mail delivery.

He loved what he did. He enjoyed his printing business not only because it provided him with a good income, but also because it allowed him to distribute his writing and opinion pieces at a time when this was hard to do. This laid the groundwork for his future as one of America's founding fathers and one of the greatest citizens of the country.

He was not afraid of hard work. He attributes many positive things in his life to the reputation he earned as a diligent, hard-working man.

He was obviously a great communicator. All you have to do is read some of his writings to be convinced of this.

He had good skills and experience that he developed on his own. He himself attributes his business success to his love of reading and writing.

He also realized how important physical fitness was. Swimming was his chosen activity as it strengthened his aerobic conditioning as well as his arm muscles. He shunned beer (that's one strike against me!) and preferred water because he had seen the ruinous effects of too much strong beer on his compatriots.

Benjamin Franklin also had his faults, which he talks about eloquently in his autobiography. If you are interested in the life story of one of the greatest small-business owners that ever lived, I strongly suggest you read his autobiography. (You can do so on the Internet by Googling "autobiography of Benjamin Franklin.") He learned what he needed to know by reading — you can too.

● ●

3

WHAT DO YOU WANT TO DO?

Okay, you definitely want to take the leap and start your own small business. Now comes your first big decision: What type of business are you going to create?

You could decide to provide consulting services on your own, out of a home office, or run a bed-and-breakfast or a home day-care. Some people have coined the term *microbusiness* to describe these types of ventures. They are examples of the simplest form of business, and if that is your long-term objective, that's fine.

On the other hand, perhaps you'd like to create a corporation that will eventually have annual revenue of millions of dollars and raise capital from the public for further expansion. That's fine too; it will just take a lot more time and effort to reach your goal.

There are myriad variations in between the microbusiness and the publicly traded corporation. Maybe you just envision a service business with one location and one employee (like mine is at this point). Or perhaps you'd rather set up a partnership with someone else, a partnership that strives for half a dozen employees. Maybe you'd like to have a store with several locations and dozens of employees.

It doesn't matter what type of business you want to build. The key is to realize that the stage you are at now, the planning stage, is crucial. Every hour of work you do now will go a long way to ensure you meet your goals.

Remember, you are no longer an employee being told what to do at every turn. You will be the owner and will have to make all the important decisions, and the first key decision you'll have to make is what business to start.

"A RESTAURANT SOUNDS GOOD"

I often hear people dreaming about starting their own restaurant, and I'm not sure why they do. I've got nothing against eating establishments — heck, my wife and I even talked about starting one a few years ago. Okay, we were sitting in a beautiful restaurant in Florence, and we'd had a couple of bottles of wine, but it sure seemed like a good idea at the time!

However, even though starting and running a restaurant sounds exciting, it has got to be one of the toughest things on earth to do. My conclusion is that many people suffer from the "grass looks greener over there" syndrome. They think that because a restaurant is such a pleasant place to eat, it would be a nice business to run. They have no idea of the risks involved in developing a restaurant and the effort required to keep it running. That's like judging a book by its cover — don't do it!

Let's look at another type of business that often attracts people who want to work for themselves. Many years ago I investigated a company that sold household water-purification products. The company made slick presentations to groups of people, telling them how much money they could make selling these units to friends and family. The presenters said anyone could make $30,000 or more each month with hardly any effort. Sounds pretty good, doesn't it?

When I arrived at the company's head office, I was amazed at the buying frenzy going on. I stood beside two individuals who I was sure knew nothing about the product or how to sell it. They handed over a certified check for $5,000 for a number of products. I have no proof, but I'll bet most of those products are still sitting in their garage.

These two examples show how easy it is for people to imagine that the grass is greener on the other side of the fence. They hate their job and have found what looks like a fun or easy way to make more money than their current salary, but without the boss or coworkers they hate. The problem is they have no idea what is actually involved in running the business. In most cases, a business that sounds easy is not. You are much more likely to succeed — and to avoid wasting a lot of time and money — if you stick to what you are really interested in and skilled at.

SOMETHING OLD? SOMETHING NEW?

For many people, the type of business they are going to start is obvious: it's what they have been trained to do. The landscaper starts a landscaping business, the doctor becomes a general practitioner, the lawyer starts law firm, and the contractor starts a construction business or provides general handyman services. This is the simplest route to take and generally has the highest chance of success because the individuals already know how to do the work of the business. It isn't a guarantee of success, however, since there is more to running a business than just doing the work (remember my description of the three-legged stool in Chapter 2?).

But maybe you'd like to do something different. Maybe you're after a change, a challenge, something you've always dreamed about spending your time doing. Now is your chance to explore that dream. It's a chance to make a change in your life that gives you the ultimate satisfaction — doing what you love every day.

Let your mind wander for a bit. What are you keenly interested in? What are your hobbies? Maybe there is a business opportunity here. Let the following stimulate your thoughts:

- *Listen to your friends and business associates.* Simply keeping your eyes and ears open is one of the best ways to find a new business idea. Listen to the people you respect. Ask them for their ideas. Is there a service or product they need that they aren't getting?

- *Think about your education and experience.* What are you good at doing? Maybe you have a knack for selling to customers. That opens up huge opportunities. You aren't limited to what you are selling now — think about what else you could apply these skills to.

- *Have a look at what others are doing.* The Internet is great for this type of research. Don't forget to look at what is going on in other countries as well. Maybe the answer is a variation of what you are currently doing rather than a major change.

- *Keep current on news and trends.* Maybe your business can offer a product or service that is not available yet but will be in demand in the future. For example, there is an aging population in North America, and a large number of baby boomers are approaching retirement. What are they going to need?

RESEARCH, RESEARCH, RESEARCH

Once you've decided what it is your business will do, it's time to determine whether anyone will buy or use what you are offering. This may sound obvious, but in many cases of business failure, the owners skipped this step. They invested a lot of effort trying to build a business before they discovered nobody wanted the product or service.

The result is a lot of wasted time, energy, and money. It can often mean the ball and chain of personal debt after the venture fails.

You need to look at potential customers and the competition, and you also need to consider how demand for the product or service will change in the future. This is easier if you are currently working for a company that is in your chosen industry already.

Just keep your eyes and ears open. It's much more challenging if you are entering an industry you have little experience in.

In either case, start by exploring the many free sources of information: industry trade journals, government agencies and departments, your local board of trade or chamber of commerce, newspapers, and magazines. The Internet makes this task much easier than it used to be, but don't forget to visit the library and ask for help. I am always amazed at how helpful librarians are — it's surprising what you can find out merely by asking. (Self-Counsel Press has also published a number of helpful books, including *Market Research Made Easy*, by Don Doman, Dell Dennison, and Margaret Doman, which explains what research you need to do and how to do it. Also look for Self-Counsel's "Start & Run" series, which gives specific information for people thinking of starting a variety of small businesses.)

One thing to consider carefully when determining the potential demand for a product or service is whether you are going to sell to businesses or to individuals.

If you are going to market your services to businesses, start by analyzing the market of your competitors. Are the clients in a solid industry? If your clients are on shaky financial footing, you run the risk that you will not get paid. Research the industry and the companies within it before deciding to service it.

If you are going to sell to individuals, the best way is easy and cheap: let your friends, family, and associates know what it is that you have to offer and sit back and see if anyone asks for it. If they do, you're onto something. If they don't, it's not the end of the world. Do more research by asking why they aren't interested: it's free information from people who usually give their unbiased opinions. That type of information is invaluable.

• •

Learning from Hollywood

Because I have the entrepreneurial itch, I'm always on the look-out for it in the people and events around me. It can be truly inspiring when you see it.

I found a great example, literally the night I wrote this section. It came as I was watching a movie — one of my favorite pastimes.

The movie was *In Her Shoes*, based on the novel by Jennifer Weiner. It's an engrossing tale of two completely different sisters who eventually learn to appreciate one another. What caught my eye was that both sisters have the entrepreneurial itch. Rose (Toni Collette) is a workaholic lawyer who happens upon a business as a "freelance dog walker." No real research done at all — she is walking a dog that was left at her house, and people who know the dog's owner ask her how much she charges. She sets up a deal with a kennel to refer clients to her in exchange for half of the fees. It helps her create a life she actually enjoys after she quits her stressful job.

Maggie (Cameron Diaz ... wow!) is a scatterbrained party girl who visits her grandmother Ella (Shirley MacLaine) in Florida on a whim. She ends up helping one of Ella's friends buy a new outfit for a special occasion. Another woman asks Maggie if she would do the same for her and offers to pay for her help.

"Do you think there's other women down here who would?" Maggie asks Ella. "Are you kidding? Scads," is Ella's response. Maggie says she's thinking of "doing it like a business." Ella's response? "Well, that's an excellent idea." Maggie admits she isn't good with numbers, to which Ella replies, "Well, I'm good with numbers. I could help. If you like." "Yeah, sure, that'd be good," Maggie says, and a business is born. Within days, the lineups start — Maggie is busy full time and finally has a direction to her life and money in the bank. I love movies with happy endings like this!

• •

While you're researching the business you want to start, you should also keep the following questions in mind:

- *Do you enjoy doing the work?* It is a lot easier and more satisfying if you choose something you enjoy doing. Don't make your decision purely for financial reasons or you may find yourself giving up before long.

- *Will you be getting repeat business?* If your services are needed only once or infrequently, you will constantly need to bring in new clients to maintain your current profitability. That means you'll spend a lot of time and effort marketing your business. It is much easier to run a business where your clients will need your services over and over again.

- *Is there a franchise available?* If you are interested in getting into a business you know little about, you may wish to consider purchasing a franchise. These businesses already have a proven record, so your chance of success increases dramatically. I'll explore franchises in detail in Chapter 12.

- *Could you volunteer at another company to gain experience?* My first employee became my first employee because he called and offered to work for free. This posed little risk for me, as all I had to invest was the time it took to train him. He was good at his job, so after only a few weeks I started paying him for his work. This may be something for you to consider if you don't have much experience in your new business.

THE BUSINESS PLAN

Once you have decided what product or service you are going to offer, it's important to continue the planning process. Put your thoughts down on paper in the form of a business plan. This does not have to be a 100-page document. It could be an informal summary of your intentions for the business that fills less than a dozen pages.

A business plan is also not set in stone. Most of the people I know who created a formal business plan did not stick to it. Many did not even bother to update it after they got the business up and running. The point is that it's the best place to start. The more time and effort you spend documenting what it is that you are trying to accomplish, the greater your chances of success. You may even find, during this process, that you come up with a better idea than the original product or service you had decided on. Or you might see additional opportunities arising from your original idea.

Besides describing how you intend to market your product or service, the business plan should include the following information:

- A description of the products or services

- A summary of the start-up costs

- A projection of sales and expenses for at least the first few years

- An analysis of your own strengths and weaknesses — will you need help with some aspects of the business?

- An analysis of the industry — is it steady, declining, or growing?

- A marketing strategy — how do you plan to find customers or clients?

If you are planning to establish a large entity that will require external financing from banks or possibly investors, your business plan will need to be formal and detailed. You will probably require the assistance of a lawyer, an accountant, and possibly a business adviser. It will be difficult to obtain financing if you have not researched and documented all the details of how the business will work. (Keep in mind that no matter how well-written a business plan may be, you may still be turned down by the bank. See Chapter 5 for more information about financing your business.)

It's easy to find sample business plans on the Internet. I just Googled "business plan templates" and got over 42 million hits. Look for examples of award-winning plans. There are many available, and some may even deal with your specific product or service.

• •

Elements of a business plan

A good business plan is concise and written in plain language. It contains charts, illustrations, and graphs placed appropriately. It uses realistic assumptions about future income and expenses and provides detailed information in appendixes.

It should include the following basic components:

- *Cover page.* Include the company name, address, telephone and fax numbers, website URL, and email address, as well as the names of key company contacts.

- *Table of contents.* Summarize the major sections of the plan.

- *Executive summary.* Write a brief (one- or two-page) summary of the major points in the plan.

- *Company summary.* Include the company's goals and its objectives as well as the amount of financing required.

- *Management.* Summarize the experience and qualifications of all key people who will be involved.

- *Marketing strategy.* Outline your market research, the strategy for attracting customers or clients, and the pricing strategy (i.e., will your products/services be inexpensive or premium priced?).

- *Financial projections.* Set out what start-up costs you will incur, and include five-year income-and-expense projections and a loan repayment plan.

- *Advisers.* Include the contact information of your lawyer, accountant, and other advisers.

- *Conclusion.* Summarize your goals and objectives, the required financing, and the reasons why this is a good investment.

- *Appendixes.* Include detailed management résumés, any product illustrations or literature, any financial statements, detailed cash-flow forecasts, and any major customers or clients you may have.

RESEARCH SHOULD NEVER END

Once you've started your business, don't stop thinking about what changes you'll need to make to keep it viable. A product or service that is in hot demand today may be collecting dust on store shelves tomorrow. Think of film processing. Ever since I bought my digital camera, I haven't touched my 35 mm film camera. Those companies in the film production and processing industries that did not anticipate this change are no longer around.

Even in a service business, it's crucial that you keep thinking about the specific services you offer now and what you will be offering in the future. This is known as identifying your niche.

NICHE TODAY, GONE TOMORROW?

Dictionary.com offers one definition of niche as "a situation or activity specially suited to a person's interests, abilities, or nature," and another as "a special area of demand for a product or service." If you wish to build a satisfying business, it is well worth taking the time to identify what your niche is going to be. But be careful. Relying on one niche could spell the end for your business.

This was made clear for me during the dot-com boom of the late 1990s. At the time, it seemed that things were going a little crazy. People with no business experience were starting Web-based businesses and becoming millionaires within months. That sounded cool, and I wanted a piece of it. I spent a lot of time developing accounting systems and solutions solely for dot-com start-ups, and I knew several other accountants who were doing the same thing.

What would have happened if I had neglected my existing clients and put all my eggs in the dot-com basket? I would have lost my client base and replaced it with clients who, in most cases, soon ceased to exist. In a matter of months, good clients with investors pouring money into their businesses would have become bad clients unable to pay their bills.

Having one niche is beneficial, but risky. If you happen to choose an area that suffers a severe downturn, you may be in trouble. That is why it may be best to work on developing at least two niches.

What is good about a niche?

One of the main advantages of developing a niche for your business is that word-of-mouth naturally occurs if what you do is specific and unique, and that is what people are more apt to remember. Because you have defined exactly what products or services you offer, it's more likely that you will come to mind when these people happen to talk to other people who could use what you offer. That may be reason enough to establish your own specialty, but there are other advantages:

- *The learning curve is faster.* It takes you less time to investigate issues relating to new clients because you will already be familiar with many of the problems that they may have. If you take the time to document policies and procedures for dealing with clients in a manual, new employees can refer to it instead of having you continually investigating and explaining things to them. This could save you and your employees significant amounts of time.

- *You decide what type of work you do.* Because you have spelled out your niche, you will attract work of your choosing rather than simply accepting what comes your way. Take my case, for example. I have been an accountant for over 20 years and have wrestled with the issue of identifying my niche for much of that time. Accountants do many things, but I have found that people often assume we are all tax specialists interested in doing personal tax returns. Over the years I have tried to dispel this notion because it is not an area I want to be involved with.

- *It is easier to keep current.* Trying to keep up to date on many different types of businesses at once is time-consuming. If you specialize in one area, it is much easier to keep current.

Always be thinking about your next niche

It is also important to remember that establishing a niche should not be a static process. You should constantly be thinking about changing your current niche and perhaps adding new ones so that you don't get caught flat-footed as client demands change.

Over the years I have always been on the lookout for new niches and considering what my next niche should be. Here's just a partial list:

- Doctors

- Women entrepreneurs

- Engineers

- Incorporated businesses

- Dot-com start-ups

- QuickBooks accounting set-ups

- Training in software

- Tax minimization

- Nonprofit audits

- Notice-to-reader accounting engagements

I've finally arrived at a mix of niches that I enjoy. This process of constantly reviewing one's current niches and thinking about other ones has allowed me to phase out of a traditional accounting practice and focus on other areas that I enjoy more and that I find more profitable. Here are my current niches:

- *Small business* — reaching out to small businesses by writing books, articles, Web content, courses, and other material, and participating in speaking engagements

- *Personal finance* — writing, lecturing, and speaking on behalf of organizations including banks, learning institutions (including universities), and government departments whose mandate is to help individuals handle their personal finances and prepare for retirement

- *Accounting and taxation for small service businesses*

- *Outsourced accounting work* — providing outsourced functions, including internal audit functions, to government and other organizations

□   □   □

Now is your chance to dream a little. What is it that you'd love to do for the rest of your life? Can you make good money at it while enjoying more time off? Your choice of business may be obvious if you enjoy what you do, but it doesn't have to be. Be logical and don't rush. Now is the time to invest in your future — a future that could be your dreams come true.

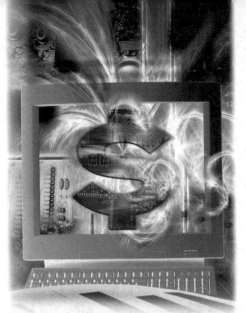

4

IF YOU CAN SELL, YOU'LL DO WELL

Say you've researched your business, planned how you are going to run it, decided on a couple of niches, and are ready to roll. Where are you going to get your first client or customer?

I don't know the specifics of your education, but in my years of high school, university, and accounting school, no one ever taught me how to sell. I can't think of one course that was available through the education system that addressed this essential skill. Without some selling skills, your business will likely be dead in the water.

So how did I figure out what actually brings in clients and customers? I learned it the same way I learned most of my small business lessons: by trying things out myself and by seeing my clients succeed and fail.

WHAT DOESN'T WORK

Let's begin with the things I tried that sound completely logical but that didn't work for me. Then we'll move on to what I do now that does work. As you'll see, they are almost complete opposites.

The mailing list

Buying a mailing list or email distribution list of potential clients sounds like a good idea. You could develop a flyer showcasing your particular skills and get it into the hands of hundreds, perhaps thousands, of potential clients. If you use snail mail, you spend a bit of money to buy a mailing list, print a flyer, and mail it out. Email is even cheaper — just the cost of the list and perhaps the cost of hiring someone to send out the message. What could be simpler, right?

The problem is that, for a lot of businesses, sending out a flyer can be a waste of time and money. For example, the most common source of clients for professional services is personal referrals. Think of how you found your doctor, dentist, or other professional. You probably asked trusted friends or acquaintances who they use, right? That's because you wanted to know if the service provider was any good before you entrusted your health or personal information to them. I tried sending out flyers in the beginning, but I found it ineffective.

On the other hand, it *does* make sense for some businesses to distribute flyers in this way. For example, a hairdresser or a retail shop will want to contact as many potential customers as possible before opening day. Such businesses will need to reach beyond the owners' personal contacts to build up a sufficient client base. It makes sense to deliver flyers to residences and businesses in the neighborhood. It sometimes makes sense to use a mailing list to connect with more people. The key is the quality of the mailing list. It has to be current, and it has to target the business's core audience.

Expensive one-time advertising

A client I had many years ago was trying to break into the area of logo and website development. Four people had set up the business, and they had already signed an office lease before I met them.

They paid $1,000 for a one-time, half-page ad in a large daily newspaper. The paper served a population of over two million people, so a lot of eyes passed over the ad. How many calls did they get? Zero. I remember how shocked they were. Shocked and $1,000 poorer.

That business did not last two years. What's worse, the four individuals were left with a large amount of personal debt because they had put so much money into the business to get it started and keep it going.

It wasn't just the lack of selling and marketing knowledge that caused them to fail. The actual creative and design skills were sadly deficient as well, but the fact that they lacked any experience in selling was a major contributor to the business's downfall.

Advertising works; it just takes time. People need to see an ad more than once for it to register. Perhaps the best advice is to start slowly and try other, less expensive methods in the beginning. Then, when your business is up and running and generating cash, and you want to take it to the next level, try placing advertisements. But make sure you develop a well-targeted campaign of sufficient duration.

Newsletters

I tried sending out newsletters for years. In the beginning I sent them out by fax. Later I distributed them by email. I put a lot of time and effort into them. They did not just provide the latest tax or accounting tips that bore everyone to tears. The focus was helping small businesses grow, and the tips were based on my own experience (much like this book). I diligently gathered business cards everywhere I went and carefully added them all to my computer's contact management system, which served as my distribution list.

I must have spent at least a dozen hours a month developing the content, adding names to my contact manager, and actually doing the broadcast fax or email. People often commented on how interesting the content was, and when I stopped sending them a few people even noticed that I had stopped and asked me why.

But I honestly can't remember getting more than a few new clients as a result of the exercise.

Build a website and they will come

You've heard the pitch: "Let us develop a cool website for your business. Get access to billions of potential clients!"

After I stopped sending out newsletters, I took all the content I had developed and created a website at www.MyWebCA .com. I registered with all the search engines. I made sure all articles I wrote for any other publication, whether print or web-based, referred people to this site for further information.

I carefully tracked the statistics. In a good month I recorded 10,000 to 15,000 distinct visitors (not just hits). And yes, the website brought in some clients. But notice how I said *some* clients, not hundreds, not even dozens. Here's the kicker: most of the clients were the nondesirable ones — the price shoppers. In fact, for one I did the work and did not get paid.

Don't get me wrong here — I am not against a small business having a website. In fact, I would encourage you to investigate getting one. The cost is quite low, and a website can be a real asset. It can help people find you. In fact, I create a new website for every book I write. (This book's site is www.entrepreneurial itch.com. Check it out.) It's a way for my readers to get in touch with me to let me know what they think. I get many testimonials and ideas for future books through the Web. But I don't expect it to bring me customers.

WHAT WORKS (FOR ME)

Okay, let's move on to the cheap and effective things that have actually worked for me.

Personal contacts

Let me start with how I got three of my latest clients:

- *Coffee shop.* After dropping our two kids off at school on a Wednesday at 8:30 a.m., I went to my regular coffee shop to recover from the trauma of actually getting them to school on time. At the shop, I ran into a couple whose child used to go to the same school as my son. We chatted about how their son was doing, and they mentioned they were working on course development at an organization that was creating a curriculum on personal finances. They said they'd send me the name of the individual who was in charge of hiring writers. The next day I got an email with the contact information. My friends had already discussed my qualifications with this person, and they told me he wanted me to call. I phoned him on Friday, we met the next Wednesday, and I was hired two days later to develop a chapter for their course.

- *Seminar.* At a recent educational seminar on personal financial planning, I volunteered to speak about tracking personal spending and documenting net worth. During the break after my presentation, a lawyer came up to me, introduced herself, and told me she had a wealthy client who needed the service I had just been talking about. I gave her a business card on the day of the seminar (Friday), and the client called the next Thursday. She brought in her financial records the Thursday after that.

- *Existing client.* One of my long-time accounting clients had to elect full-time officers for their organization of approximately 1,600 members. As an accountant, I was already in a position of trust and was asked to administer the election. No selling necessary.

In my experience, personal relationships are the best means of attracting new clients. Granted, I have been in business for almost 20 years, am a published author, and have a contact database with about 900 names in it. Since you are just starting out, it will be more difficult. The point is to start thinking about who you already know and begin with them before you consider paying money to see if you can attract people you don't already know.

The story of my dentist

Here's another real-life story that happened a decade ago and made it clear to me how important personal relationships are to the business-building process.

My dentist's wife, Linda, worked full time in his office, booking appointments and handling the administration. She was also in charge of the marketing efforts and was always trying new things to attract and retain patients. She knew I was an accountant and asked if I was aware of a recent tax rule change regarding dental expenses. I said I was, and she asked if I would produce an informative brochure on the change for her husband's patients. I could put my full contact information on the brochure, and I thought it would be a good marketing tool for my accounting practice.

I produced the brochure, and Linda displayed them prominently on the front counter. Guess how many calls I got from potential clients.

None.

Yes, that's right. I didn't get one call in response to the actual brochure.

Here's the interesting part, though. Linda was on the board of directors of an organization that was looking for a new accountant. I became the accountant for this organization, and I billed annual fees of $3,000. I also got another client out of this — a company that subleased the second floor of the organization's building. Total annual fees — over $6,000. All from the personal relationship I had developed with Linda.

OTHER KEYS TO MARKETING YOUR BUSINESS

There are several other lessons about marketing a business that I have learned the hard way. Here they are:

- *Repeat business is key.* I repeat — repeat business is key. If the clients keep coming back year after year, as they do in an accounting practice, you'll be able to spend much less time looking for prospective clients. A specialized consulting firm that is constantly looking for new business by responding to requests for proposals (RFPs) will be spending a lot of time and money on that activity, which may ultimately bring in no new clients or income. If you can, offer a service that clients will need over and over again.

- *Follow up with potential clients.* At any given time, I probably have half a dozen potential clients who have made the effort to get in touch with me about providing services to them. In the early years it is especially critical that you follow up with each and every one of them. Don't get sidetracked trying to bring in fresh new clients and customers — deal first with the ones who are already in the door.

- *Go for lunch.* You have to eat lunch anyway. Why not do it with a potential client or referral source? Taking someone for lunch is an effective way to spend quality time with them. It's a little thing that can go a long way toward building a relationship. Remember the client that spent $1,000 on an ad in a large newspaper? Think of how many lunches that could have paid for.

- *Just pick up the phone.* I often find that a day or two after I talk to a person I haven't been in touch with in a while, I get a call from someone they know, inquiring about my services. That's because I am on my contact's mind for at least a few days after our conversation. If you are on someone's mind, chances are he or she will identify situations that you could become involved in. It's easy to do — just pick up the phone and call someone you haven't talked to for a few weeks or months. I know it's easier to send an email, but that's also easier to ignore. A phone call is better because it's more personal.

- *Practice selling … or get someone else to do it.* Selling doesn't come naturally to me. As a result, I have hired other people to do it for me. This never worked out in the past because even though these people knew what they were doing, they didn't really understand what I was offering. I now have an associate working with me who does get it. He and I collaborate to target potential clients, and he uses his experience and skill to sell them my services.

Now that you've considered the various methods of attracting customers and have some idea of what might work for you, it's time to take the next step — actually starting the business. This is the stage where many people make mistakes, often fatal ones that doom the business before it can bloom. You only get one chance to start a business — make it count.

● ●

Learning from an expert: Alex Woda

I have never met anyone better at selling and marketing than my friend and client Alex Woda. Alex is not a formally trained marketing expert. He is an MBA and an information technology (IT) consultant. But what Alex does brilliantly is sell.

Alex founded his company, Alex Woda and Associates Inc. (AWA), in 1993 as an IT consulting firm specializing in IT audit, security management, and training services. AWA has a staff of professional information-system auditors and security specialists who help organizations manage operational risk. My firm has provided accounting services to AWA since the start, and I have been privy to the ups and downs of its development.

Secrets of Success

As long as I have known Alex, he has believed that developing a specific niche is the key to growing a company. He has never been just a general "computer consultant"; he is a computer security specialist. AWA's mission statement is: "To provide exceptional consulting services and software solutions for risk management, information system security and information technology audits. We achieve our mission through knowledge sharing, project management and developing software solutions to facilitate and enhance the processes of risk analysis and control."

Now *that* is a niche! Alex has found that focusing on his niche produces the following advantages:

- *Referrals/word-of-mouth.* His existing clients are most likely to think of him when they come across an associate who may need his services.

- *Expertise.* Alex and his staff can focus their time and energy on keeping themselves up to date on the issues affecting their niche. As a result, they offer better service.

- *Training.* It is easier to train staff in one area than to bring them up the learning curve in a variety of areas, including ones they have never encountered before.

There is a risk, however. As I mentioned in Chapter 3, if you choose a niche that suffers a major setback, your business may be in trouble. Computer security is unlikely to suffer in the future, however, since the threat of hackers, viruses, and other problems will probably exist as long as people use computers.

Alex's Four Rules for Success

Great companies don't just happen. They are the product of hard work and the person or people in charge who know what they are doing. Alex attributes his success to the following four basic rules:

1. *Make the client look good.* If you make your clients look good to their customers or perhaps their boss, do you think you will get further business from them? What if you make them look bad? Obviously, if you make them look good, they are more likely to call you back. Remember, the easiest way to grow your business is to repeatedly sell your products or services to your existing clients.

2. *Take work off your client's hands.* If you start a job and leave the client with a long to-do list, you have just added to his or her problems. Admittedly, there are often tasks that clients must do themselves, but if there are things that you can look after, it will make their lives easier and often will allow you to continue your work to completion (and billing) sooner.

3. *Give your client more than he or she expects.* You may have heard the phrase "underpromise and overdeliver." This is the same concept. People are used to being overpromised and underdelivered; if you do the opposite, you will not be forgotten soon.

4. *Have fun!* Seriously, this is important. Who do you think will be more successful, someone who loves what they do so much that they would rather do it than sit and watch TV with a beer in hand, or someone who hates going in to the office?

Just like the owner of any growing business, Alex has overcome, and continues to face, numerous obstacles. Finding good staff is a constant challenge, as is developing a marketing and image strategy for the company. Long-term planning is another area that continually raises concerns. Like life in general, running a small business is a process, not a destination. If you enjoy the ride, the destination is irrelevant.

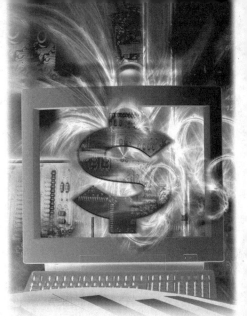

5

GIVE YOURSELF A CHANCE: START ON A SHOESTRING

The best advice I can give anyone setting up a new business is to start on a shoestring budget. That means you should focus a lot of your energy on keeping costs down.

The type of business you are getting into will obviously make a huge difference. A consultant working out of home will require a lot less start-up money than someone opening a retail clothing store in a mall.

The clothing store owner will need to rent space for the store, buy inventory (clothing) that will be displayed for sale, hire sales associates, etc. This is a major commitment that involves major risks. What if the business is not successful? Can you afford to be left with thousands of dollars of debt and with other commitments (a lease on the store, for example)? I'm not saying you should not open a clothing store, but if you do, carefully consider the risks you are taking on. Unless you already have a lot of experience in retail clothing sales and have managed a store similar to the one you envision, you would be wise to defer a decision to open a retail store until you have the necessary experience and financial backing. (If retail is for you, check out Self-Counsel's *Start & Run a Retail Business*, by Jim Dion and Ted Topping, as well as other books in the "Start & Run" series.)

THE HOME OFFICE

If you are trying to keep costs down, it only makes sense to start working out of your house or apartment. Committing to pay office rent before you know your business will succeed is like dropping a brick on your foot before a marathon race. Why make it harder on yourself than it already is?

Advantages of a home office

I started out in a home office myself. There were many advantages other than the low cost, including the lack of a commute. The ability to go from breakfast to full-out working in less than two minutes can't be beat.

Many clients prefer that you go to them and would rather not be forced to come to your office, so it doesn't matter whether you have a fancy office and boardroom or not. In fact, after I moved out of the home office to a downtown tower, I actually lost a client, largely because he now had to come in to town to see me.

Another advantage is the ability to claim a tax deduction (subject to certain conditions) for your home office. This is the best type of tax deduction available — the one that makes the expenses you already have deductible.

Disadvantages of a home office

A home office is not perfect, however. Maybe your business *will* require you to bring clients or customers to your home for meetings. Some may not care, but it's often a different story for large corporate clients. It's not so professional when your cat knocks a cup of coffee into the CEO's lap.

Depending on your personality, you may also find it difficult to keep focused. The fridge and television are only a short distance away at all times! This wasn't a big problem for me because I can focus without being distracted. In fact, I am writing this very chapter in my home office (which I kept). It's easier for me to focus here than in my other office with the phone ringing and people dropping by.

The other disadvantage I found was that I could never get away from the business. Even after-hours and on weekends, I could always drop by the room that served as the office to check messages or do some administration. As a result, I found myself burning out because all I thought about was the business. That's not healthy.

START-UP COSTS

If you've decided to start a consulting or service business out of your home, you won't have the burden of office rent, but you will still have some costs. Let's look at them now.

You'll probably need a computer, office supplies, Internet access, business cards, and maybe a cell phone and PDA, among other things. These items can't be avoided. There is, however, a more significant cost that many people don't consider: personal living expenses during the start-up phase.

It is reasonable to assume that it will be weeks, possibly months, before any revenue begins to flow into your business. This is because it will take time for you to establish your business, meet and attract clients or customers, get your first job or sell your first product, produce an invoice, and receive payment. During this time you'll still have to feed your family. The length of time between starting up and getting the first payment is the reason many small businesses fail soon after they are launched — too much is expected of them too early.

This is also why it's a good idea, if possible, to start your business part time while you still have a job. It eliminates the pressure on you to make a profit too soon.

If you have a service business, keep in mind that there is a time delay before your clients actually pay you. Say you bring in a new client and the work starts in two weeks. It takes another two weeks to complete the project, a few more days to decide how much to invoice, and another couple of days for the invoice to get to your customer in the mail. Your customer (unless he or she is pleasantly unusual) will often stretch the payment to 35 to 40 days, not the 30 you asked for. Add all the days up — it is about ten weeks or two and a half months.

What are you going to do for cash during that time?

WHY NOT GET THE BANK TO HELP?

Most people think that getting a bank loan is the first step in starting a small business. It certainly sounds logical — you borrow money to pay for the start-up costs and pay it back over time as the business generates a profit. Unfortunately, it usually doesn't happen this way.

I've seen more than a few cases where an individual has spent a significant amount of time and effort creating a complex business plan with detailed sales projections, only to be flat-out rejected by the bank. And the business never gets off the ground.

This is not surprising. Banks are not in business to help small businesses grow; they are in business to make a profit for their shareholders. They are keenly aware of the statistics on new-business failures. You've probably heard yourself that most businesses fail within the first five years. Unfortunately, it's hard to dispute the facts. Why would a bank lend you money if the odds are that you won't be able to pay it back?

While I do recommend that you spend time preparing a business plan, including doing as much market research as you can, don't assume that your plan will necessarily persuade the bank to lend you the money you require. The knowledge you gain by actually doing the business plan is the key benefit you're likely to receive.

WHERE DOES CASH COME FROM BESIDES A BANK LOAN?

If the bank turns you down, where else can you go for start-up cash? You might have savings you could use; you could possibly borrow from family or friends; you might finance your business on your credit cards; or you might get a line of credit from the bank.

Your savings and "sweat equity"

If you have some money set aside in a savings account, you could put that money into the business and use it for the start-up costs. Unfortunately, most of us (me included!) don't have money lying around to start a business.

What we all do have, however, is "sweat equity" that we can donate to build the business. This means that we put our hard work, time, and skills into the business and don't take money out until the business can afford to pay us.

Think of it this way: If you could borrow money from the bank, you may feel it is logical to pay yourself for your services, since the bank loan is a source of cash for the business. Since the bank often won't advance a loan to a new business, however, you may be forced to work for free. This results in less cash flowing out of the business since no cash is available.

That's fine for the costs of your services, but what about when you have to buy office supplies and equipment? You'll need cash for these types of expenses, so you will have to consider the other main sources of money.

Friends and family

Friends and family are a possible source of cash, but this money comes with strings attached. What happens if your business does not survive and you can't pay the money back? Your friends could lose their money, and you could possibly lose their friendship. If you borrow from family, problems could surface that destroy loving relationships.

For these reasons I never tapped into this source of funds. The risks are just too high. You may think differently. That's fine — just make sure that you get the terms of any loan in writing and stick to it. Friends and family are two of the most important things in your life. You don't want to lose them in a fight over money.

Credit cards

The reality is that most small businesses are financed by the owner's personal credit cards because the credit is already available. The high interest rates on unpaid balances make this an expensive way to finance your business, but often credit cards mean the difference between starting a business and not starting one.

If you are considering using your personal credit card to pay for your start-up costs, make sure you have a bare-bones, no-frills card. It won't give you the frequent-spender points and fancy rewards of a gold or platinum card, but that's not what you need. You need a low interest rate to minimize the costs of your venture.

Make sure you treat your credit card with respect — your debt can quickly spiral out of control because it's so easy to justify buying something else on the card. Try to use credit only for the computer and other equipment you need to start the business. Avoid using it for things like advertising. It's too easy to build a balance you won't be able to pay back if you start spending on things that don't last.

The bank again

As soon as you have proven to yourself that your business will succeed, consider asking your bank to give you a line of credit based on your personal credit history. Once you receive a line of credit, the first thing you should do is pay off your credit card because the interest rate will be at least a few percentage points lower than the one on your credit card. For more on the issue of finding start-up funds, see Angie Mohr's book *Financing Your Business*, published by Self-Counsel Press.

THE CASH-FLOW CRUNCH

Sooner or later your business will run into the dreaded cash-flow crunch. The bills will come due but the bank account will be empty. As I've mentioned, this often occurs before the business has a chance to get established because people don't anticipate and plan for their continuing need for money to pay personal bills.

Unfortunately, for 99 percent of businesses, the cash-flow crunch never goes away. It is a constant worry for most businesses, small or large, throughout their entire life. I still battle cash-flow issues to this day, even with a solid client base.

At a lecture I attended, hosted by a small-business magazine, the moderator asked the top ten entrepreneurs of the year what they lost the most sleep over. Their answer, unanimously, was cash-flow concerns. Think about it. When you are just starting out, your expenses are low — you may not even have to pay rent if you work at home — but you still have to worry about cash flow. When your business grows, you may have money rolling in, but you'll need a lot of cash to pay for your office, your employees (perhaps dozens of them), and all of your other expenses. Planning ahead so you have money in the bank to meet payroll can cause a lot of sleepless nights.

I'm not going to sugarcoat things here. Running a small business, even a successful one, is not easy. It's stressful at times.

Since the cash-flow problem never goes away, you might as well learn how to deal with it now.

Tips for easing the cash-flow crunch

You've started running your business out of your home part time while retaining your job, but how else can you keep your costs down and avoid running out of cash? Consider the following tips:

- Shop around for the cheapest credit-card or line-of-credit interest rate you can get. This may be available from the bank you have been dealing with, but be prepared to go to a new bank.

- Consider leasing computers and other office equipment, rather than buying, so that you can reduce your monthly payment amount. This also leaves you with available room on your credit card or line of credit. (See the "Leasing Versus Buying" section on page 49.)

- Get at least three quotes each year on all your insurance (house, car, business, health, etc.). If you are operating out of your house, make this clear to the insurance companies to ensure your homeowner's policy provides sufficient coverage.

- Review your cell-phone and long-distance bills each month, and call the supplier to make sure you are on the best plan.

- Avoid expensive printing costs by producing your own letterhead and business cards using low-cost color inkjet or laser printers.

- Ask your lawyer and accountant for fixed-fee, up-front quotes for all services they provide. Ask them what you could do to keep their fees down.

- Use the telephone and the Internet instead of traveling whenever possible.

- Apply for a line of credit at your local financial institution before you think you need it, and before you launch your business. It is easier to get one at this time. If you do not have a banker, get to know one — as with almost anything related to small business, personal contacts are key.

- Never use cash in the bank to purchase a long-term asset (i.e., something that will last more than a year, like a computer or furniture). Unless you are making so much excess cash you don't know what to do with it, spending the money may handcuff you when it comes time to pay current suppliers, your employees, or yourself. Either lease long-term assets or take out a loan that you can pay off over the course of the item's useful life.

- Avoid writing a check that clears out your bank account. You never know when you will collect your next account receivable. Even if your customer has promised "it's in the mail," the check may take days to arrive or it may be rerouted for some reason. That puts a lot of stress on you. Hold back on paying nonessential items until that money is in your hands. This will save you many sleepless nights and embarrassing calls to good clients where you ask if you can go pick up the check.

. . . .

Leasing versus buying

Leasing is the same as renting — you pay a fixed amount per month for the use of some property or piece of equipment, and then you return the item at the end of the lease term. Leasing is becoming more and more popular as a method for obtaining computers and office equipment. For one thing, it spreads out the cash flow. Instead of paying $3,000 for a new computer, for example, you agree to pay $100 per month for three years. The advantage is clear — you don't have to scrounge for the money up front.

The other advantage is that if you don't have the cash to buy an item, you don't have to use expensive debt financing (a loan with a high interest rate) such as a credit card. Leasing is popular even for established businesses with lines of credit, because it preserves the available money on those lines of credit. The $3,000 that is not put on a $25,000 line of credit is $3,000 for the business to use for other purposes.

. . . .

Track your daily cash flow

Avoid the damage to your reputation if you bounce a check. The best way to keep track of your cash flow is to have an accounting system you can update every day. Note that this will not result in the same balance as a bank statement would show you because your system will include checks that have not yet been cashed.

If you cannot update your system daily, you will need another way to keep track of your ready cash. One easy method is to use the check stubs that come with most checkbooks. Make sure you account for receipts only when they are deposited, and record all automatic withdrawals, telephone or online banking transactions, etc.

I'll discuss bookkeeping in more detail in the next chapter.

• •

Learning from an expert: Stephen Mader

One of the most successful entrepreneurs I have had the pleasure of knowing is Stephen Mader. Stephen runs Artery Studios Inc., a medical visualization company that creates medical illustrations, animations, and interactive media primarily for the medical-legal field — including lawyers litigating cases with a medical focus, such as insurance or malpractice claims. Artery also creates visuals for the advertising, pharmaceutical, broadcasting, publishing, and patient education markets.

The company has been in business for over 15 years and currently employs 11 people in an 1,800-square-foot contemporary office space in the heart of downtown Toronto. What makes Stephen unique is his remarkable consideration for people. Whether they are customers or employees, he is always concerned with helping them meet their needs and achieve their goals. That is why, for example, his company offers employees a tailored health plan, a generous pension plan, and educational incentives.

Details, Details

Another thing that makes Stephen so successful is his attention to detail — specifically the financial details of growing his business from the ground up.

Right from the beginning he was concerned with where every dollar was coming from and going to. It probably wouldn't surprise you to learn that Stephen started planning his business while he had a full-time job. He put in a lot of hours of research during evenings and weekends before taking the plunge to go it alone.

In Stephen's case, the decision was made easier by the fact that his employer offered him a severance package because it was closing down his department. While this was a worrisome time for him (he was 29 and had just assumed some personal real estate debt), he soon realized it was a golden opportunity — the severance provided the money he needed to live on while he devoted all his time to getting his business off the ground.

Start-up Costs

Stephen took a course on starting a small business. During this course he generated a comprehensive business plan. He took his plan to the bank and asked for a $5,000 loan to buy his first computer. The business plan not only included detailed income and cash-flow projections, but even showed how he proposed to repay the money. The bank turned him down flat, and he ended up using money out of his own pocket and borrowing the rest of the necessary cash from family.

This experience ended up being a positive one, according to Stephen, as it set the standard for how he has dealt with finances ever since. He finances the business using only cash generated by the business, and he uses credit only for bridge financing for specific purchases or unforeseen expenses that just can't wait.

One other important point: when he started on his own, his life partner had a full-time job. This helped cover most of their personal expenses for the first few years of his business when cash flow was a concern, but they were still short of cash. "I spent so much time marketing, including taking on lower-paying but higher-profile work to establish my reputation," he says, "that I did not have enough income to meet our significant financial needs. So, for the first year, I took a part-time job, working at night in a related field." Stephen's dream of self-employment meant that much to him — he simply had to make it work.

Stephen's Tips

Stephen has learned by doing. Now you can learn from what he did. Here are a few of his tips — some of the most useful tips related to small business that I have heard:

- *Treat people well.* Treat them well and keep them happy by creating a culture they will appreciate. If you eventually choose to spend less and less time running your business, you'll need good people to sustain this culture while you are not there. Also, to reduce staff turnover, hire people who may not have strong entrepreneurial skills, but who will provide consistency and stability for the business and will grow as the company grows.

- *Don't expand until you need to.* Don't commit to expanding your office or staff until you are "bursting at the seams." Don't stretch yourself thin by committing to expenses you don't need or aren't ready for. It should be obvious when you need more space and more resources and when you need to hire more people.

- *Apply for disability insurance.* As a sole proprietor, apply for health and disability insurance before you need it and while you still can. Stephen applied after he left his full-time job and was initially refused insurance. The agent told him that if he had applied while he was still employed, it would have been no problem.

- *Apply for credit early.* Apply for the maximum credit-card and line-of-credit limits that you can, and try to do this before you launch your business. Even if you don't use them (Stephen has a business line of credit he has not used in seven years), they may be the financial lifeline you need, especially during cash-flow difficulties. Pay off these debts as soon as possible.

- *Set goals.* Never stop reaching for goals, even if others think they are unachievable. You may not fully realize those "over-stretched" goals, but you'll set your sights higher and go farther than you would if you went through each day without an idea of where you wanted to end up.

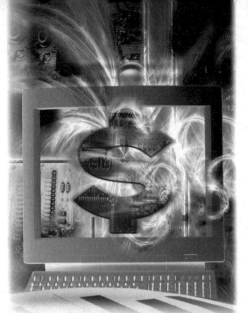

6

BOOKKEEPING: LIFEBLOOD OF A BUSINESS

Don't worry: I promise I won't bore you by going on at length about the nitty-gritty details of bookkeeping. However, accurate and current bookkeeping records are absolutely crucial to the success of your business.

Bookkeeping is not that scary a subject — it's all based on logic. You don't need to become an expert on accounting concepts and terminology either, although there are several key concepts that will help you. Let's briefly look at them now.

BASIC ACCOUNTING CONCEPTS

A basic grasp of the following terms and concepts will be very useful:

- Accrual accounting

- Debits and credits

- Financial statements and journal entries

- Equity

- Capital assets

- Amortization and depreciation

Accrual accounting

No, *accrual* doesn't come from the word *cruel*!

Accounting on an accrual basis simply means that you record income and expenses in the period they are earned or incurred. This matches the revenue to the expenses in the period to which they relate.

In comparison, recording income and expenses when they are collected or paid is referred to as accounting on a cash basis. This method does not give you an accurate picture of what happened during a period of time because a minor change in the timing of cash inflows and outflows can have a large impact. For example, assume a company's business year ends on the last day of the calendar year. If the payment for a $10,000 invoice were deposited on December 31, the company would show a profit for the year that was $10,000 higher than it would be if the payment were deposited on January 1 of the next year.

Accounting on a cash basis also leaves accounting results subject to manipulation. For example, in order to reduce income taxes, you could ask clients not to pay you until after your year-end, while you prepay your expenses. This would reduce your revenue and increase your expenses, resulting in lower net income and therefore lower taxes.

Let's consider a simple example of the difference between cash and accrual accounting. Say you started your business, working out of your home office, on December 1. Your year-end is December 31. You had one client and billed $1,200 for the work you did for that client during December. The date of the invoice was December 31. Your office supplies delivered in December cost you $200, and you paid for them with your credit card. Your client paid you the $1,200 on January 15 of the next year and you paid your credit card bill on January 23 of the next year.

Figure 1 shows how your records would look depending on whether you were using the cash or accrual method of accounting.

FIGURE 1
CASH VERSUS ACCRUAL METHOD OF ACCOUNTING

Income statement
December 1 to 31, 20—

	Cash basis	Accrual basis
Revenue	$0	$1,200
Expenses	$0	$200
Net income	$0	$1,000

The cash method implies that you did nothing during December. The accrual method shows the reality: you worked hard to bill $1,200 and you spent $200. Your profit during December was the difference, $1,000, even though no cash actually flowed during the period.

Debits and credits

In accounting terminology, *debits* (DR) and *credits* (CR) are two fundamental terms for recording transactions. Debits represent increases to assets and expenses, and decreases to liabilities, revenue, and equity accounts. Credits represent decreases to assets and expenses, and increases to liabilities, revenue, and equity accounts.

When you pay for a business expense, you would record this as a debit to an expense account (an increase in expenses) *and* a credit to an asset account (a decrease in assets like cash). When you sell a product or service, you would record this as a debit to accounts receivable (an increase in assets) and a credit to sales (an increase in revenue). One of the fundamental principles of accounting is that for any given transaction, *debits equal credits*.

Financial statements and journal entries

The balance sheet and income statement are the two basic statements included in a full set of financial statements.

- *The balance sheet* records assets (i.e., things the business owns, such as money in the bank; accounts receivable from customers; and property, plant, and equipment), liabilities (i.e., debts the business owes, including accounts payable to suppliers and credit cards, bank loans, etc.), and equity (i.e., accumulated profit and money invested in the business by the owner or shareholders). The balance sheet shows the state of the business at a point in time — most commonly the year-end date.

- *The income statement* records the revenue (also referred to as income) and the expenses for a period of time — usually the business (or fiscal) year. The difference between the revenue and expenses is the net income or profit. If expenses exceed revenue, the difference is the net loss.

In bookkeeping, a journal entry is how you record financial transactions. Remember that every accounting journal entry (JE for short) has two sides: a debit and a credit. For example, going back to the scenario described in the section on accrual accounting, if you billed a client for $1,200 on December 31, you would record a debit to your receivables account and a credit to your sales account. The journal entry for the sale would look like the one in Figure 2.

FIGURE 2
SAMPLE JOURNAL ENTRY: INCOME

Journal entry 1 (to record Invoice 1)
December 31, 20—

	Debit	Credit
Accounts receivable	$1,200	
Sales		$1,200

By selling a product or service, you increase both your accounts receivable (recorded as a debit to your assets) and your sales (recorded as a credit to revenue).

Now let's look at another example. When you purchased office supplies as described in the scenario above, you would record the expense as a debit to one of your expense accounts and a credit to your payables account. Figure 3 shows how you would record the December 15 transaction.

FIGURE 3
SAMPLE JOURNAL ENTRY: EXPENSE

Journal entry 2 (to record invoice for office supplies delivered December 15, 20—)

December 31, 20—

	Debit	Credit
Office supplies expense	$200	
Accounts payable		$200

Many people get confused about debits and credits because their personal bank statements show their withdrawals as debits and their deposits as credits. That's the opposite of what one might expect, so why do they appear that way? It is because you are looking at the bank's accounting records, which are the opposite of yours. A deposit in your business bank account shows as a debit on your balance sheet because it's your asset, but it's a credit on the bank's balance sheet since the bank owes the money back to you.

Equity

Equity is the residual interest in the assets of a company after deducting the liabilities. In other words, it's the difference between the assets and the liabilities of a company. It is shown on the balance sheet and includes capital stock (the amount paid for shares in the business) as well as retained earnings (the total after-tax net income of the business since it started).

If the business is not incorporated (that is, if it is a sole proprietorship, as in the examples above), there will not be any shares to buy. Figure 4 shows what the balance sheet for the company in the examples above would look like.

FIGURE 4
BALANCE SHEET

At December 31, 20—

Assets

Accounts receivable	$1,200
Total assets	$1,200

Liabilities

Accounts payable	$200
Total liabilities	$200

Equity

Owner's equity	$1,000
Total liabilities and equity	$1,200

The balance sheet is a snapshot of everything a business owns and everything it owes at a particular time. Notice that the total assets equal the total liabilities and equity. Every balance sheet must show this fundamental accounting equation:

Assets = Liabilities + Owner's Equity (or Retained Earnings, for corporations)

Capital assets, amortization, and depreciation

Capital assets (also called fixed assets or property, plant, and equipment) are those items a business buys that last for more than a year. Examples include real estate and office equipment such as desks and computers, as well as trucks and plant equipment. They are included on the balance sheet as assets because they are things the business owns.

If you expensed capital assets on the income statement in the year you bought them, you would have a huge expense total in that year, even though the use of the asset would extend into future years. The expense of buying the capital asset would not logically match the revenue that it will help earn in the future. This is why capital assets are *amortized* or *depreciated* (the two words mean the same thing) over time. This means the total costs are broken down and expensed on the income statement over more than one year.

For example, say you bought a computer for $1,500 and its projected life span was three years. This asset would go on the balance sheet at its cost of $1,500. However, on the income statement you would record an amortization expense of $500 for the first year. That would reduce the "book value" (the cost less the accumulated amortization since the purchase) of the computer on the balance sheet to $1,000. At the end of the second year, another $500 would be expensed on the income statement, reducing the book value on the balance sheet to $500. The third year would see another $500 expensed on the income statement, which would reduce the book value on the balance sheet to zero.

See, there is no magic here!

BOOKKEEPING FOR SOLE PROPRIETORS

A sole proprietorship is not a separate entity from the owner in the way that a partnership or a regular corporation is. If you operate as a sole proprietor, you and your business are one and the same thing. Many people who operate in this manner do not have a formal bookkeeping system to separate their business income and expenses from their personal finances. They may not think a formal system is necessary, but keeping track of your business expenses and personal finances separately is extremely important.

Recording business finances separately makes tax time easier

Tax time is usually a nightmare for people who don't separate business from personal expenses. They have to collect their tax-deductible expenses from all over the place. Perhaps some were on personal credit cards, some were paid for in cash, others were covered by a personal check or a line of credit. How can these people ever be sure they have found all their business expenses? The truth is, they can't.

If your business finances are mixed together with your personal finances, you are likely missing tax-deductible expenses and therefore paying too much tax.

Recording business finances separately gives a clearer view of your personal finances

Another advantage to separating your business from your personal life is that you have a clearer view of where your personal finances stand. If everything is mixed together, how will you know if your cash-flow problems are caused by your business or because you are spending more than you make?

If you are like most people, you don't spend much time analyzing your personal finances, even though you should. Because personal expenses are not tax deductible, they cost you a lot more on an after-tax basis than business expenses, which are tax deductible. If you eliminate unnecessary personal expenses, you will obviously end up with more money and you can therefore reduce the amount of time you have to spend working. I'm always amazed by the number of people who totally ignore this.

Let's look at an example. Say you worked hard to bring in another $1,000 in sales. Because sales revenue is taxable, you will not end up with an extra $1,000 in your pocket. If your business income is taxed at a rate of 30 percent, you will pay $300 in taxes, which will leave you with $700.

If instead of increasing your sales by $1,000, you reduced your personal expenses by $1,000, that would mean an extra $1,000 in your pocket.

Still not convinced? Look at it another way. In order for you to earn an extra $1,000 to spend on something personal, your business would need to generate $1,428 before taxes.

$1,428 x 30% = $428 in taxes

$1,428 – $428 = $1,000

That's a lot of work, isn't it?

The conclusion? Focus on controlling your personal spending as well as your business growth. Consider how you might reduce the amount you spend on credit card interest, insurance, meals and entertainment, vacations, automobiles, and mortgage interest. If you try to achieve significant savings each year on your personal finances, it will reduce the pressure on you to make more and more profit in your business.

Recording business finances separately lets you see how your business is doing

The other major problem with operating without a formal bookkeeping system is that you never get a good snapshot of where your business stands.

This can be a costly mistake. I have seen people continue to run money-losing businesses for years longer than they should have, simply because they didn't know how bad things really were. They poured a lot of money down the drain.

You are much better off if you separate your business from your personal records and track its activities with formal bookkeeping software.

ACT LIKE A CORPORATION

If you are a sole proprietor, consider operating as if you were a corporation. Corporations must keep accurate bookkeeping records and have procedures in place so they can file corporate income tax returns and keep any investors informed about the operating results.

As a sole proprietor, you need accurate bookkeeping records not just so you can file income tax returns, but also to help you run your business. Without accurate records, you are like a driver without a map trying to reach a destination in a foreign country.

The first thing you should do is open a separate business bank account. Once you have a separate account, use it only for your business deposits and expenses. It is much easier to track all the cash flowing in and out of your business if it is confined to one bank account. In order to track the cash, buy a bookkeeping software program designed to do this. Don't use a spreadsheet — you will only end up pulling your hair out as you try to get all the numbers you need from it. If you are not willing or able to do your own bookkeeping, it is a wise investment to hire someone part time to help.

BOOKKEEPING MADE EASY

I am keenly aware that most of you are not bookkeepers and may never become number crunchers. However, you ignore this function at your own peril. If you don't pay attention to it, your business is almost guaranteed to fail.

The good news is that bookkeeping doesn't have to be a chore. A good, low-cost bookkeeping software package can help you run your business as it takes care of a lot of the details behind the scenes.

The package I use is QuickBooks from Intuit, but Simply Accounting from Sage Software or Microsoft Dynamics GP are just as good. The price of these products starts at less than $200 — possibly the best investment a small-business owner could make.

If you use your bookkeeping software to produce your invoices and process your checks, you'll have taken a large step toward generating accurate financial information.

Invoicing and accounts receivable

When you use your bookkeeping software to produce your client invoices, it will record a bookkeeping entry as soon as you generate an invoice. The entry will automatically show the sale amount and will also track the receivable from the customer and any taxes that were charged.

If, on the other hand, you use a word-processing program to produce an invoice, you'll then have to remember to enter each invoice into whatever accounting system you've set up. This creates more work and adds the element of human error to the equation: you could forget to enter the invoice and might not notice if you did not get paid.

The next step is to use the bookkeeping system to record every check or other payment you receive from each customer. The system will then produce one of the most important reports of all: the accounts receivable aging report. This lists the amount each customer owes and how long they have owed it. You can easily send copies of the invoices directly from this report to customers by email, reminding them that they haven't paid yet. Using your bookkeeping system to control the payment process is the best way to control your cash.

Paying bills

Many business owners write out each check. They then must enter each check in the bookkeeping system. This adds an extra step and increases the possibility of errors at the writing and entering stage.

It's worth getting preprinted company checks (i.e., with your company name and address on them) and using your bookkeeping software to print the checks. This has the advantage of automatically entering the checks into your accounts payable records. Prerpinted checks may cost less if you get them from an office supply store rather than from your bank. You should also consider mailing checks to suppliers in double-window envelopes. This eliminates the need to produce a mailing label when you are sending out payments.

Other bookkeeping entries

If you diligently use your bookkeeping software to issue invoices and write checks, you will automatically have recorded all your sales, cash receipts, and expenses paid by check. That may be 70 percent or more of the entries that are required.

All that will be left for you to record are expenses paid using other sources such as credit cards, cash, telephone and Internet banking, automatic withdrawals for things such as computer leases, etc. If you can enter these items yourself, that's great. Keep in mind that hiring a bookkeeper to come in once a month or once every quarter to fill in the missing information is a lot cheaper than having him or her do all your bookkeeping.

A word about using spreadsheets for bookkeeping

If you are handy with computer spreadsheets, this may seem like a good way to track your income and expenses, but for business bookkeeping purposes I strongly encourage you to resist the urge.

When you use a spreadsheet, you may be able to record all the ins and outs of your bank account, but you will not be able to summarize and group all the transactions into their respective categories. Nor will you be able to print checks, generate invoices, and easily display valuable information such as a list of accounts receivable from clients. All this can be done automatically by bookkeeping software, but it would be virtually impossible to customize a spreadsheet to do this.

If you use a formal bookkeeping system, the double-entry requirement will ensure that you record all revenue and expenses that flow through your business bank account. If you miss something, your accounts will not balance. For example, if you use your business bank account to pay for all your expenses, the month-end balance on the bank statement should be the same as the bank balance in your accounting system. If they are not the same, you should be able to explain why they don't match. This is called *reconciling*. Reconciling the bank balance in your accounting system with the bank statement may indicate when you have not entered items such as bank charges in your accounting records. A spreadsheet makes it harder to track these inconsistencies.

Of course, if you pay for a business purchase with cash and then lose the receipt, that transaction won't be recorded as an expense nor will you get the tax deduction. This is why I recommend that you use a business bank account for as many expenses as you can.

SETTING UP YOUR BOOKS

Setting up the books is one of the hardest parts of getting your small-business accounting records working properly. If you use an accountant, consider asking for help. You only have to do the set-up once, but if it's not done properly, it will lead to inefficiencies and extra costs later on if you have to pay a bookkeeper or accountant to correct things.

Bookkeepers versus accountants

An accountant is not the same thing as a bookkeeper. A bookkeeper is someone who enters the financial information in the bookkeeping system and reconciles the accounts to make sure all entries have been made properly. He or she should be able to produce "internal" financial statements from the bookkeeping system to help you run your business.

An accountant is someone who prepares "external" financial statements — those that would be presented to your banker, for example — and your business's annual income tax return.

If you are just starting out, it's a good idea to have at least an initial discussion with an accountant to make sure you have chosen the most appropriate business structure and set up the bookkeeping records correctly. This will also ensure you have someone lined up to prepare your income tax returns at the end of your first year. If you don't already know an accountant, ask your friends and fellow business owners who they use. You probably won't use an accountant's services much in the first year, but once you become established it will help make sure your business files the necessary financial and tax forms. You don't want to get on the wrong side of the tax authorities — it can turn your dream business into a nightmare.

The chart of accounts

Most bookkeeping software packages come with templates for setting up your basic accounting categories or chart of accounts. Often there are a variety of preset charts of accounts for different businesses. Instead of getting an accountant to set it up for you, you could choose the template that most closely resembles your business.

After you set up your basic chart of accounts, customize it as necessary. Start by deleting the accounts you know you'll never need and adding ones that you will.

Since one of the most important functions of your accounting system will be tax reporting, it makes sense to set up the expense categories that the government requires. In the United States, you will be filling out a Schedule C, "Profit or Loss from Business" form. In Canada, the equivalent document is Form T2124, "Statement of Business Activities."

Schedule C — Profit or Loss from Business (US)

Sole proprietors in the United States are required to report their expenses in the following categories:

- Advertising

- Car and truck expenses

- Commissions and fees

- Contract labor

- Depletion

- Depreciation

- Employee benefit programs

- Insurance (other than health)

- Interest — mortgage

- Interest — other

- Legal and professional services

- Office expenses

- Pension and profit-sharing plans

- Rent or lease — vehicles, machinery, and equipment

- Rent or lease — other business property

- Repairs and maintenance

- Supplies

- Taxes and licenses

- Travel, meals, and entertainment — travel

- Travel, meals, and entertainment — deductible meals and entertainment

- Utilities

- Wages

- Other expenses

- Expenses for business use of home

Form T2124 — Statement of Business Activities (Canada)

Sole proprietors in Canada are required to report their expenses in the following categories:

- Advertising

- Bad debts

- Business tax, fees, licenses, dues, memberships, and subscriptions

- Delivery, freight, and express

- Fuel costs (except for motor vehicles)

- Insurance

- Interest

- Legal, accounting, and other professional fees

- Maintenance and repairs

- Management and administration fees

- Meals and entertainment (allowable part only)

- Motor vehicle expenses (not including capital cost allowance)

- Office expenses

- Property taxes

- Rent

- Salaries, wages, and benefits (including employer's contributions)

- Supplies

- Telephone and utilities

- Travel

- Other expenses

Group your expenses

An alphabetical listing of expenses, while fine for income-tax-reporting purposes, is difficult to analyze because the list is so long. To make the data easier to study, group the expenses by category. There are, arguably, four main groups:

- *Administration.* This encompasses the cost of running your business, which includes office rent, telephone charges, office supplies, insurance, legal and accounting fees, software, computer costs, travel, etc.

- *Cost of sales.* This category includes the direct costs of the product your business sells, including the cost of inventory, production wages, etc.

- *Marketing.* This can include meals and entertainment, advertising, the website, gifts, etc.

- *Operations.* This category covers the other costs of doing business, such as dues and subscriptions, computer leases, travel, etc.

Each group is made up of the individual expense accounts. The following list shows one possible way of grouping the expenses required on Schedule C (excluding cost of sales), by category:

Administration

- Insurance (other than health)
- Interest — mortgage
- Interest — other
- Legal and professional services
- Office expenses
- Rent or lease — other business property
- Repairs and maintenance
- Supplies
- Taxes and licenses
- Utilities
- Other expenses
- Expenses for business use of home

Marketing

- Advertising
- Commissions and fees
- Travel, meals, and entertainment

Operations

- Car and truck expenses
- Contract labor
- Depletion

- Depreciation

- Employee benefit programs

- Pension and profit-sharing plans

- Rent or lease — vehicles, machinery, and equipment

- Wages

Here is the list of expenses required on Form T2124, grouped by category:

Administration

- Bad debts

- Business tax, fees, licenses, dues, memberships, and sub-scriptions

- Insurance

- Interest

- Legal, accounting, and other professional fees

- Management and administration fees

- Office expenses

- Supplies

- Telephone and utilities

Marketing

- Advertising

- Meals and entertainment (allowable part only)

- Travel

Operations

- Delivery, freight, and express

- Fuel costs (except for motor vehicles)

- Maintenance and repairs

- Motor vehicle expenses (not including capital cost allowance)

- Property taxes

- Rent

- Salaries, wages, and benefits (including employer's contributions)

- Other expenses

The tax forms do not require you to separate the expenses by category, but doing so gives you some sense of the big picture without bogging you down in the details. For example, knowing that you've spent a total of $84,000 on expenses is much less informative than seeing it broken down into categories like this:

Administration	$16,000
Cost of sales	$32,000
Marketing	$15,000
Operations	$21,000

You'll see the importance of this level of detail when you focus on the key numbers and try to improve the bottom line, as we'll discuss next.

FOCUS ON THE KEY NUMBERS

Once you have your bookkeeping system set up and are keeping your records current, you should focus on several key figures. This list is not exhaustive, but keep an eye on the following, as a starting point:

- *Sales.* Compare your sales (or gross revenue) this year to last year's results and to this year's budget.

- *Accounts receivable.* Keep a close watch on what your customers owe you, especially those who pay late. If you don't follow up on old balances owing, you significantly increase the chance the customer will not pay at all. That can threaten your business's cash-flow lifeline.

- *Expenses.* Analyze your main expenses so you can target the ones you can reduce. For example, minimizing administration expenses will allow more funds for essential marketing activities.

- *Bottom line.* What is your net income before tax? Are you making enough money to satisfy your needs? If you aren't, you need to make changes sooner rather than later. Doing the accounting often triggers people to take such action.

IMPROVING THE BOTTOM LINE

There are only a few ways to improve your bottom line. Basically, you can increase your revenue, decrease your costs, or better yet, do both.

Increasing revenue

As you start out, you will likely find that increasing sales is difficult. This is because you don't yet have a large client base to which you can offer additional services or an extensive network of contacts from which to get referrals. Also, you will still be learning which selling techniques work and which ones don't. Out of necessity, you'll need to be cost-conscious.

Cutting the right expenses

When you are considering what costs to cut, think about the four main categories of expenses, and decide which ones are most crucial to your business. Let's look at each in turn.

- *Cost of Sales — Products.* If your business sells something tangible, you'll obviously have to buy the product before you can sell it. The trick here is not to buy before you know you will be able to sell. If you commit to buying a large amount of inventory and then end up being stuck with the product, it can ruin your company. Try the Dell Computer method of buying inventory "just in time." Dell only orders the products or raw materials after the customer has placed the order. And, needless to say, it gets the best price it can.

- *Cost of Sales — Services*. For service businesses, the product is not a physical commodity but something intangible. If you do all the work, your primary cost of sales will be what you pay yourself. If you hire staff, however, the cost of sales will include the cost of your staff. Remember, though, that most service businesses don't have work nicely smoothed out over the year. You'll have busy periods when you'll have to work weekends, and you'll have slow periods when you'll wonder if you'll ever get another job. Resist the urge to let your staff go when things are slow. If you work hard, sooner or later things will pick up, and if you have no staff you won't be able to service your clients.

- *Administration*. Administration expenses are necessary, but they don't directly contribute to your bottom line. You should try to minimize expenses in this category, but there are certain things you can't avoid, including business licenses, membership dues, insurance, interest, legal and accounting fees, office supplies, telephone charges, utilities, and office rent.

- *Marketing*. Many people reduce marketing expenses to save money. When things get tight, it's easier to eliminate advertising than, say, rent. Often the entertainment budget (meals with clients and so on) goes out the window. The problem is that doing this stunts the growth of your business. For instance, if you lose touch with your existing and potential customers or clients, you may cut off your ability to bring in new business. The key is to avoid cutting *effective* spending in this area while being careful not to incur costly but ineffective marketing expenses.

- *Operations*. This category encompasses the other costs of running your business, including computer and equipment leases (or the depreciation on these items if you purchase them), courier and travel expenses, and wages for employees other than those in administration and directly involved in manufacturing or providing the service. These costs are often higher than administration and marketing, and therefore warrant close consideration and ongoing monitoring.

KEEPING CURRENT IS KEY

Once you have a bookkeeping system, make sure you keep it up to date. Accurate information isn't much use if it's too old. I have seen dozens of businesses fail, and the one symptom common to most of them has been the lack of current and accurate accounting records. If your business is to survive and thrive, you must know where it stands at all times.

Okay, you've survived the chapter on bookkeeping — congratulations! If this chapter makes sense, resolve to improve your bookkeeping skills by taking a course or reading a book on the subject (as I mentioned in Chapter 2, Self-Counsel Press has several great books by Angie Mohr). If it all seems like Greek to you (and you aren't Greek!), set aside a budget to hire a bookkeeper, or seek an associate who has those skills. Without good bookkeeping, you are putting your whole business dream at risk.

7

AIM FOR THE IDEAL BUSINESS

While it is impossible to create the perfect business, it's useful to think about what one would look like. This idea can then dictate the kind of clients you look for, the amount of work you do, and the type of niche you carve out, among other things.

THE IDEAL CLIENT

The key factor that will determine whether your service business is something you enjoy or something that constantly drives you nuts is the clients you end up with.

The less desirable ones are difficult, always demanding attention and action, and complaining when things don't go their way. In the beginning, as you work to attract clients, you will likely have to accept some in this category. Good clients are hard to find, and if you turn the bad ones away, it will be hard to pay the bills. As your business grows, however, you'll want to weed them out. One of the joys of a growing business is the ability to dump a client who is a total pain in the butt.

But what exactly makes clients ideal? Good clients exhibit some or all of the following characteristics:

- *They are low maintenance.* Ideal clients respect your opinion and value your time. They don't ask for your home phone number (unless, of course, it's the one you use for business) so they can call you anytime of the day or night to discuss the smallest issue. They also understand that you'll need time off for vacations and won't try to track you down during that time.

- *They don't complain about your fee.* Most people are concerned about what they pay for goods and services because they only have a finite amount of money. You can't fault people for trying to keep the fees they pay you to a minimum. The problem is with clients who constantly complain about your fees and are always nickel-and-diming you, trying to get you to charge less. If you have many clients of this nature, your life won't be much fun and you won't make much money. An ideal client will readily pay a reasonable fee without complaint.

- *They actually pay on time.* There is nothing worse than putting in a huge effort for a new client, sending out an invoice, and then never getting paid. This is categorized as a bad debt expense on your income statement. You billed for the work done so it's recorded in your sales, but the client never pays the invoice so an offsetting expense has to be recorded. These people are often the same ones who complain about the invoice in the first place. Ideal clients always pay their bills on time. I have several ideal clients, whom I love — in some cases they cut me a check as soon as I present my invoice to them.

- *They are profitable themselves.* Let's face facts — if your clients are not making money, it will be hard for them to pay your invoice. (I cover this in more detail in the next section.) This is a problem I faced when I provided accounting services to some not-for-profit organizations. The staff at these organizations were almost always nice people, and they worked hard to provide needed services, but many of them were just scraping by. It's difficult when you provide services that are worth $2,500, and the client can only afford to pay you $1,000. As my practice grew, I decided to reduce the number of smaller nonprofits on my client list so I could free up my time to serve larger clients from whom I could recover full fees.

The stage of your business is a factor here. When you start out, you may have to accept clients that can't pay full fees. You may even decide to volunteer your services to one or two organizations in order to get the word out about your business. This can be an effective way to meet people who will refer you to new clients in more profitable industries. Just be careful. Consider the ability of each prospective client to pay your fee — before you accept them as clients.

Pick and choose your clients

Obviously your ideal business will have a client base made up only of good clients. It's not easy to achieve this, but it is possible.

The trick is to have so many potential clients coming to you that you can afford to take on only the good ones. You're unlikely to be able to pick and choose when your business is just getting off the ground, but I have found that the longer you are in business, the easier it becomes.

I am now busy enough doing the type of work I love to do that I do not feel obligated to return each and every email or phone call I receive from potential clients. If it looks or sounds like someone will not be a good client (and it gets easier and easier to determine this from their phone or email message), I don't bother to get in touch with them.

Make sure your clients are in a solid industry

If you can select the types of businesses to pursue as clients, you might want to focus on an industry that is flourishing now and will probably continue to do so in the future.

If your clients are in businesses that aren't stable and profitable, you'll have constant headaches as they pressure you to charge lower fees and are tardy with payments. This isn't necessarily because your clients are bad people but because their companies are having cash-flow problems. If your clients have cash-flow problems, so will you.

If your clients are in a strong industry, they will have less trouble paying their bills. You will also benefit from the following:

- *Less time spent on marketing.* You'll spend less time trolling for new clients because your existing clients will be around year after year.

- *Faster learning curve.* If you're working for the same clients repeatedly, or for clients in the same industry, it will be easier to keep up with relevant business issues. This also makes it easier to train new staff.

- *Your business will grow.* Your clients will probably be growing in size and will likely need more goods or services from you. Trust me, your life will be a lot easier if you have one client who pays you $15,000 a year than if you have 15 clients who pay you $1,000 each.

GET OTHERS TO DO THE WORK

The ideal business is one in which the owner (you) doesn't have to do all the work. In fact, if it's truly ideal, it would continue to run even when you are not there. That is only possible for most businesses if there are employees.

The decision to hire someone is often a difficult one. You will be taking on responsibility for paying someone's salary, and that raises several questions. Can you afford it? How much can you afford to pay? Where do you find someone good? There is also the issue of where they will work — do you want them coming into your home office? Or will they work remotely out of their own home office, or will you need to rent an office for them?

While I am not a human resources expert, I will try to shed some light on the financial side of the issue and on what I've learned from my personal experience as an employer.

What kind of help do you need?

There are myriad tasks involved in running a small business, from selling to strategic planning, to administration, bookkeeping, and filing taxes. You are probably good at some of the tasks and not so good at others. I have found that most people tend to do what they enjoy and what they are good at, putting off more unpleasant tasks for later (or never). Perhaps you are great at selling and marketing but not so good at administration. Maybe you are great at providing services but not so good at bringing in new clients. Maybe you need help with the actual services you offer. The point is that you should look at those critical areas that are not being attended to — they are likely the areas you could use help with.

When can you afford to hire someone?

As you grow, you are unlikely to arrive at a point where you say to yourself, "Gee, I have all this extra cash lying around. Maybe I should hire someone now." Making the decision to hire someone involves a trade-off between what that person will cost and the profits you will earn because of the help. Generally, you are better off hiring a person on a part-time basis before taking the leap of hiring a full-time employee. This will result in a gradual increase in your costs and will give you the opportunity to see how well the person performs and whether he or she fits into your business.

If you hire someone on a part-time basis, you can generally pay him or her on an hourly basis as an "independent contractor." That keeps it simple — you pay this person as you would any supplier. Most independent contractors will send you an invoice for the number of hours worked multiplied by their hourly rate.

Once you take the step of hiring a full-time employee, your life will become more complicated. Employees cost you more than independent contractors because of government benefits you will be required to pay.

Administering payroll is another problem. You will need to compute the deductions, forward them to the government, and file the annual pay slip. Most small-business accounting software include a module that takes care of payroll for you, but make sure you subscribe to the payroll update service that keeps the tax tables current.

If you are a neophyte at bookkeeping and payroll, or if you just want to save time and hassle, you may wish to hire a payroll service company that can take care of the calculations and paychecks (or direct deposits), the remittances to the government, and any regular employee filings, all at a minimal cost.

COMPETING WITH YOU IS DIFFICULT

If it's easy for someone to start a business just like yours, you'll soon have competitors vying for your clients. If you have lots of competition, you'll face the prospect of losing customers and clients to anyone willing to charge lower fees. Let me give you a couple of examples.

Several years ago my local grocery store introduced a prepackaged meal called "Butter Chicken." It was amazing and delicious. The whole meal, including basmati rice, was ready after five minutes in the microwave. It was so popular that it often sold out. But a funny thing happened. The original product disappeared off the shelf one day, to be replaced by the grocery store's own no-name brand. I'm sure the store simply sent it out to tender to be produced by the lowest bidder. The company that first made the product is probably out of the loop.

I have also lost business to a competitor recently. A client I'd had for about five years wrote me a letter, thanking me for my services and informing me that the company had chosen to go to another accountant who was willing to charge less. That's one of the problems with traditional accounting services — it's easy to compete.

In both these cases, I don't think there was much that could have been done to keep the business or the client. The Butter Chicken people could not compete with a no-name manufacturer, and I was not willing to do a $5,000 job for $3,000. As I suggested earlier, aim to create a business that you can differentiate from competitors by offering quality goods or services that can't easily be duplicated.

YOUR WHOLE FAMILY IS NOT TIED UP IN THE BUSINESS

In some situations, husband, wife, and children all work in the same business. This can be a great way for the family to be together and enjoy one another's company. On the other hand, it can lead to tension as work and personal issues permeate life 24 hours a day.

Another problem is that all the family's eggs are in one basket. If this business goes under, the entire family's well-being is at stake.

Perhaps the ideal situation is to have one spouse run his or her own business while the other has a full-time job elsewhere. When you first experience the up-and-down nature of cash flow in your own business, you'll appreciate having a steady paycheck coming in. Ideally the full-time job will also offer benefits, including a health plan and possibly a retirement savings plan or pension.

COULD IT BE WEB-BASED?

The Internet has the potential to be the backbone of a great business. You could have a great Web-based business if the following describes your product or service:

- There is worldwide demand for it.

- Your customers can't buy it around the corner.

- It can be easily shipped — perhaps over the Internet (e.g., software or something in electronic form).

- You can accept payment by credit card.

The success of iTunes shows that even music can be sold online. Books, especially electronic books, are also being sold successfully. The problem is that not a lot of products or services seem to be perfectly suited to the Internet. Obviously, consulting services don't meet all these criteria and neither do traditional goods.

Perhaps the ideal solution is a business that combines bricks-and-mortar with the Internet. You significantly expand your horizons if you combine the ability to sell locally with the international markets accessible via the Web. If you have a suitable product or service, try selling it in your own community and then leverage the knowledge from that experience to expand your sales online.

▣　▣　▣

You are at the formative stage of your business. Before you make a final decision about what to sell, think about what your business will look like when it gets to where you want it to be. It will be time well spent. You're not likely to achieve perfection, but having an image of your ideal business will give you a goal to aim for. It will also help you when you're making those day-to-day decisions and struggling to keep things moving smoothly, even on bad days when things threaten to spin out of control. In the next chapter I'll suggest a few techniques for maintaining control.

8

RUN YOUR BUSINESS; DON'T LET IT RUN YOU

I'm not going to sugarcoat this. You will have good days and you will have bad days. I still do, and I'm sure it will continue. On the bad days, the computer will break down, you'll lose a client, or you'll be tied up in a meeting that is not earning you any money. Maybe you'll miss a client deadline, or that proposal you spent days on will be rejected by a potential client. With luck, all these things won't happen on the same day!

On the other hand, you will have good days too. You'll get that great new client you've been pursuing. The big check you've been waiting for will arrive. You'll get a phone call from a client who asks if you'd be interested in a cool assignment. Or maybe you'll have worked hard for weeks and earned a few days off to spend at the amusement park with your kids.

Treat the bad days for what they are — just bad days. Focus your energy on trying to produce as many good days as you can. The best way to do this is to spend time actually shaping and controlling your business rather than letting it grow like a weed.

JUGGLING THREE BALLS AT ONCE

In Chapter 2 I talked about business as a three-legged stool. In order for the business to be stable, there must be three fundamental aspects — operations, selling and marketing, and finance and administration — and all three must be of equal importance. If you are starting out alone, however, even if you've developed all three necessary skills, you may be wondering how the heck you do all three at the same time. This question touches on one of the biggest challenges of running your own business: it takes a lot of time and effort.

I remember what it was like when I started out on my own as an accountant in 1988. I had a small client base and was looking for some hourly work at a larger accounting firm that would help me pay the bills and also allow me to gain experience in the business. The few days I was offered quickly turned into almost a full-time job, as the firm was successful and had many clients. Over the next year I worked 1,750 hours on chargeable work with clients.

Let's work through the numbers. With two weeks off, that was fifty 35-hour weeks of client work. That was the operations leg of my stool, and it was good for my pocketbook, but when did I do all the necessary selling, marketing, finance, and administration? On evenings and weekends, that's when. In fact, I only had time to perform the most basic finance and administration duties. Selling and marketing fell by the wayside.

You might be able to predict the results. I was totally burned out by the number of hours I was working; I let my business stagnate; and I became reliant on this firm for my livelihood. I had worked myself back into a job.

At this point the senior partner offered me a share of the partnership. It was tempting, as I was sure the money at this firm would be better than my income if I remained solo, but I ultimately turned down the offer.

Then the senior partner and the second-most-senior partner left the firm, and you can guess where that left me. I was out on my own with a puny client base and no hourly work. The next few years were not easy, as I struggled to find work to pay the bills while trying to attract my own clients. I even tried buying another accountant's practice. That did not work out.

So here I am now, on my own, having built my client base from scratch and having learned along the way how to maintain the three legs of the stool.

For many people, the finance and administration leg is weak. They're happy to work on operations, since that's what they're familiar with, and maybe on marketing, because they recognize the importance of getting more clients, but then they discover they haven't written an invoice for two months or haven't kept their accounting books up to date.

Since administration has always been one of my strong points, I have devoted a great deal of time to improving it in my business. One tool I have produced along the way is simple to use and indispensable for the efficient management of my business. It's my business dashboard.

WHAT'S ON YOUR DASHBOARD?

When you are driving your car, there is basic information you need — speed, fuel level, and perhaps a map to guide you. If you don't have this information, you risk getting into an accident, running out of gas, or getting lost.

You also need some more general information for the longer term — for example, your odometer reading will help you determine when to get a new car.

Imagine that your business is a car and you are the driver. What information do you need in front of you on a daily basis as you drive your business?

You'll need financial information, such as how much money is in the bank, and contact information for your customers and clients. You'll need a to-do list, a calendar, and more "big picture" information such as your business plan.

So where do you store this information, and how do you access it? You'll have financial information using your accounting software, and maybe your customer contact information, along with your calendar and some to-do lists, using information management software (such as Microsoft Outlook). The handheld units available today (including the BlackBerry, Palm Pilot, and Pocket PC) have gone a long way to help small-business owners cope. The ability to have your whole contact list and daytimer in the palm of your hand and to easily back it up on your PC at the press of one button is one of the greatest things since the microwave.

But what about the other basic information you need, such as lists of things to do this month, in three months, in one year; reports on current client work outstanding or sales to fill; data on potential clients to follow up with or marketing strategies to implement; and so on? This is not the kind of information you can easily store or access on a handheld device.

My dashboard

My personal solution is a Microsoft Excel spreadsheet that I call "MyDashboard.xls." I use it for storing all the information that my contacts database and accounting system do not contain. It is the first file I open every morning. Figure 5 shows a sample shot of the main screen.

On the first page, I can see cells A1 to H33. On that screen I have areas titled "To Do Monday," "To Do Tuesday," etc., and "To Do Next Week," "To Do Key," and "Outstanding Regular." I can see all of the items under these categories at one time and can easily cut and paste, delete, add, or rearrange items as I see fit.

When I scroll down my dashboard, I find other useful information, including the following items:

- Current work to finish (I list the client name, project, and invoice amount)

- Current work to bring in (this is work that is due soon but not in the door yet)

- Billings by client for the last three years

- Billings by client to date and projected billings for the rest of the year

- List of website and other passwords

Another benefit to having all this information in a spreadsheet is the ability to arrange items using the "Sort" function in Excel. For instance, you can sort clients alphabetically, by billing amount, by year-end, or by type of client. This makes it easy to rank your clients from highest to lowest fee, say, or perhaps by due date to determine the order in which the work should be done. In my case, I perform accounting work, I speak and write on small business and personal finances, and I offer general financial consulting services. It's a simple matter for me to rearrange my client list to determine, for example, how much revenue each type of work is producing, information that will determine the direction of my future marketing efforts.

FIGURE 5
MY DASHBOARD

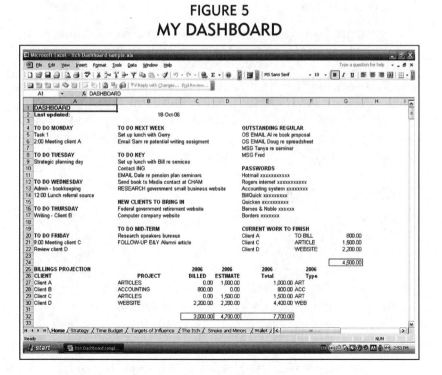

Other useful information

I have also found it useful to use the "Sheets" feature in Excel. An Excel file is actually a "workbook" that can consist of any number of sheets. The default number of sheets is three, but you can add or delete sheets at any time. You can label each sheet and access them by clicking on the tabs along the bottom. (Think of the tab dividers you would find in a binder.)

I have sheets for "Strategy," "Time Budget," "Targets of Influence," each book I am working on, and "Wallet," which contains information for everything in my wallet. (If my wallet were stolen, all the phone numbers I'd need to replace my credit cards, identification cards, etc., are in this one place.)

I used to keep this information in various paper folders and computer files in different programs, but I have found that centralizing the information into one Excel workbook is the key. This is especially true when it comes to doing the tasks you don't enjoy, because they stare you in the face until you get them done.

If you are putting together your own dashboard, think about the key information you need to run your business, and try not to duplicate information. If it's in another system (your contacts database, accounting system, etc.), don't put it on your spreadsheet. Having a dashboard can help ensure things don't sneak up on you; it forces you to take action well in advance. Experiment and try different ways of setting up a dashboard — it may help you run your business more smoothly.

THE EARLY STAGE

When you are just starting out, your biggest problem will probably be finding clients and customers to generate enough cash to get the business going. You'll also have to keep them happy. For example, when you take some time off with your family, who is going to handle emergency client calls? You may have a colleague who can cover for you, but in many cases you'll still need to check phone messages and email yourself.

Here's an example. On my last vacation, I was having dinner in a restaurant when the fellow sitting at the next table answered his cell phone. He spent a full 20 minutes with a disgruntled client who was complaining about the cleaning job his company had done. Then he had to call his employee to try to resolve the problem. Here's the kicker: He was trying to have dinner with his new bride. The two of them were on their honeymoon. See, I told you that you'd have some bad days when you were self-employed!

THE GROWTH STAGE

As soon as you move beyond a one-person show, running your business will become even more challenging. You'll have to worry about hiring staff, bringing in enough money to pay the bills, and dealing with more and more clients and customers. It's at this stage that many small-business owners let things get out of hand. They let the business control their life: They try to do everything themselves, they accept whatever clients come their way, and they work seven days a week. They don't run their business so much as they let it run them, as if it were a river they've fallen into and they're drifting wherever it takes them. The problem with this strategy is that a river sometimes ends at a waterfall.

Don't let this happen to you. Try to shape the business so you don't have to be there every day. When you start employing staff, make sure you hire people who constantly improve their skills so eventually they can perform the functions that otherwise you would do. Develop manuals that describe how to do the repetitious tasks. In short, run the business, don't let it run you. Only then can you achieve the real freedom of owning a business that makes money for you while you relax on a beach.

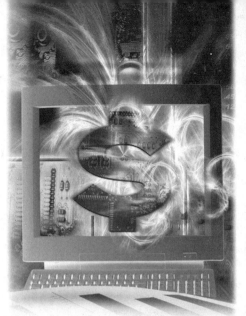

9

IT'S NOT THE TIME,
IT'S THE EFFORT

By now you've probably figured out that running a small business takes a lot of time. The days often end before the tasks do. But it's not enough to just work hard; you have to work efficiently if you want to make good money on your own. Working efficiently and charging enough for your products or services determines whether you'll succeed financially. Many small-business owners don't spend enough time thinking about pricing, so let's take some time to consider this vital issue right now.

If the business you plan to start sells products, you will base the price on what it costs you to buy the product. That cost is then "marked up" to cover overhead costs and a profit margin.

You can use a similar method when it comes to charging for services. If you have employees or subcontractors, you begin with the person's hourly wage and mark up the rate to cover overhead and to provide you with a profit. But how much do you charge for your own time? You don't have an hourly cost, so you can't base it on that. Does it even have to be based on hours?

This issue is key to whether you thrive or just survive in your own business.

THE GOOD OLD HOURLY RATE

Most professionals who bill for their services track the time they spend on each client and multiply that by an hourly rate to determine how much to invoice the client. This method is used by most lawyers and accountants, as well as many types of consultants.

Hourly billing has been around for a long time and has become the standard method of billing for services, mainly because it is so simple.

The other advantage to hourly billing is that, in most cases when you take on a job, it is impossible to predict how long it will take. If you estimate that a project will take you ten hours and tell the client that you will do it for $1,000 (ten hours at $100 per hour), you will lose money if it actually ends up taking 20 hours. Depending on how you look at it, you're either making $50 per hour for the whole project or you're working ten hours for free. In this situation, if you tell the client your rate is $100 per hour and you work until the project is done, you will make $2,000.

DISADVANTAGES OF HOURLY BILLING

There are, however, many disadvantages to billing by the hour. It may be hard to get around some of them, but it's useful to find out what they are.

It focuses on hours, not results

If you were paying someone to solve a problem, would you be willing to pay more to a consultant who toiled for hours and hours searching for an answer than you would pay to a consultant who gave you an answer in six minutes?

Think about what you do. One brilliant thought that occurs while you are taking a shower may be worth more to your client than 50 hours of painstaking research. However, if you have committed to bill by the hour, you are washing good money down the drain. You can only bill for one-tenth of an hour (six minutes) — at $100 an hour, that's $10 — while your competitor who takes 50 hours to arrive at the same solution makes $5,000. It doesn't make sense.

The point is that hourly billing doesn't reward creativity and ingenuity. It rewards inexperience and inefficiency.

It limits the amount of money you can make

With hourly billing, the client generally assumes all the risk of the job going over budget or of unforeseen circumstances arising. While this provides you some safety, it leaves no room to leverage the job into a better moneymaker. That means you will never recover more than your hourly rate. It imposes an artificial ceiling on the amount you can bill.

I'm reminded of the joke about the repair person who is summoned to an international courier company's main depot. The sorting line has ground to a halt and the entire system has been shut down. The company is losing millions of dollars a day. When the plant manager describes the problem over the phone, the repair person realizes she has encountered it before and immediately provides a quote: "I can fix the problem today for $15,000."

"Okay," says the plant manager.

The repair person arrives at the depot, walks to the central station, gets out her screwdriver, gives a certain screw a quarter turn, and, voilà, the line hums back to life.

The plant manager, surprised at how easy it was to fix, complains about the fee. "How come you charged $15,000 for only a few minutes worth of work?" he asks.

"I'll provide the details on my invoice," says the repair person.

When the invoice arrives, it includes the following breakdown:

Attendance at plant to turn screw	$50
Knowing which screw to turn	$14,950
Total due	$15,000

The trick is to know how long it will take you to complete the task before you commit to the billing method. (See the section Hourly Billing Versus Set Fees later in this chapter.)

Billable hours become more important than business growth

When you focus on billable hours, you tend to lose perspective on the rest of your business. The most important statistic becomes chargeable time. You reward yourself for production and forget that you need to spend time on the other legs of the stool — marketing and administration.

This becomes clear to many small-business owners after they complete their first big job. They have been so busy putting in the hours that they have ignored spending time cultivating the next client. The result? A good invoice going out this week, but no work to do the next.

This is what happened to me the year I did 1,750 hours of chargeable work. It was a great year financially, but I was in trouble when that work ended because I had not spent any time marketing for other work.

It treats customers unequally

If all customers are charged the same hourly rate, some will be overcharged and some will be undercharged. For example, if one customer pays $1,500 for an issue to be researched and resolved, what should you charge the next customer with the same issue? Hourly billing would suggest that the same solution costs more for the first customer than the second because the job took longer the first time. Doesn't make much sense, does it?

Also, be careful which projects you take on. About six years ago I researched a very specific issue for a client. He talked me into reducing my fee (yes, he was a nonideal client) with the argument that other clients would eventually seek the same advice. You can guess what happened — no other client ever did.

It doesn't reward the "finding" function

Tracking your hours will separate your time into "finding," "minding," and "grinding," which are alternate names for the legs of the stool — selling and marketing, finance and administration, and operations, respectively. The latter is where chargeable time resides, since you can't generally charge clients for administration or marketing activities.

If you put too much emphasis on chargeable time, though, the functions of finding and minding get shoved down your list of priorities.

It penalizes technological advances

Does it make sense that your revenue should go down if you invest money in new technology, like state-of-the-art hardware and software? With a strict adherence to hourly billing, this could happen. Improved technology lets you do things in less time, so you end up charging your clients for fewer hours.

As a result, many businesses perform routine tasks over and over in the same old way and are reluctant to develop systems and procedures to perform the tasks more efficiently. That's crazy.

HOURLY BILLING VERSUS SET FEES

Despite all the disadvantages of hourly billing, you may still have to do it this way because that's what many clients expect. This is the case for service businesses such as law, bookkeeping, and many types of consulting. In my accounting practice, I have tried for years to figure out how I could switch to fixed fees rather than charging by the hour. Believe me, nothing would make me happier than not having to keep track of the hours.

Unfortunately, I have found that I would be making less money if I didn't track them. As I have stated above, if you agree to bill your client by the hour, you impose a ceiling on your fees — you can't charge that client more than your hourly rate multiplied by the number of hours you work — but what happens if this total cost is high? In many cases, the total time value comes to more than I can recover because there's a limit to what clients think the work is worth, and they will not pay more than that amount. You will have to accept whatever they end up paying you.

Let me explain using a simple example. Say you worked ten hours at $75 per hour. The *time value* of the work is $750 (10 hours x $75 per hour), but if the client will only pay $500 for it, you have to write off the difference — $250 ($750 time value less $500 billed). It's important to note that this is not an expense to you; it is basically lost revenue. Since it is not an expense, which you would otherwise pay for out of your bank account, it does not get tracked in the accounting system. Time value, however, is something that needs to be tracked. (We'll get into this in detail in the next section.)

Not surprisingly, I find I'm usually writing off time value on the projects I do for less desirable clients, since they are the ones who complain about fees and nickel-and-dime me at every turn. With good clients, I can often explain exactly why the fee is as high as it is because I have detailed records of how long each task took (this is why you want to track your hours). Often, when I review my hourly time records as I'm creating an invoice, I am reminded of all the small tasks I also had to do for the job. Without detailed records, I might have forgotten about them, and might not have charged the client for those hours.

Setting an hourly rate

So how do you set an hourly rate?

You can start by finding out what your competition is charging. If you are going to start a bookkeeping service, for example, you could ask potential clients what they currently pay for bookkeeping. Say you find that most bookkeepers in your town charge $20 per hour. You then need to decide if you are going to match the going rate, cut your price, or *value bill* (more on that below). While it may be tempting to undercut the competition to bring in new business, I'd advise you to avoid this strategy. You'll end up with a lot of work, but you won't be making good money. You'll also find that it's extremely difficult to raise your rates, and if low prices are the reason you got the clients in the first place, you're likely to lose them when you try to charge more. You'll be stuck with the reputation as a price-cutter.

Instead consider value billing. Charge *more* than the competition and emphasize the quality of your service. You'll obviously have to be good at what you do, but you'll end up with a more satisfying business (and more leisure time to enjoy life).

Also remember that you are not constrained to one hourly rate. You can charge different rates for different functions to different clients. For example, if a rush job comes in on Friday and is due on Monday, you'll have to put time in on the weekend, which means you should try to bill a premium rate. On the other hand, if it's the middle of the summer and you have no other work when a big job comes in, you may decide to offer a small discount to get the job. In a nutshell, be flexible, but develop the confidence to bill what you are worth.

Going beyond time

Once you have gained experience in your business and can project how much time it will take to do a job, try quoting a fixed fee. Beware, though. This only makes sense if you are absolutely certain there are no elements that will make the job more difficult or time-consuming than you expected.

For example, say a new client has asked for a report on a topic you have already spent a lot of time researching for another client. The work you have done also has value to this new client and should appropriately be billed to them as well.

Even if you quote a fixed fee, however, it is still a good idea to track your time, even if it's just for yourself. This will help you to make more accurate quotes in the future, or perhaps increase your fixed fee.

Value points

Would you be interested in a solution that falls between billing by the hour and quoting a fixed fee, with the benefits of both? Try tracking *value points* instead of tracking billable hours. Think of it as tracking your "brain value."

Here's how it works. Let's say that in the last six minutes you came up with a brilliant solution that will save your client

$5,000. The client realizes the value of your solution (it's easy to show him — it's worth $5,000) and should have no problem paying several hundred dollars for it. If your hourly rate is $100 per hour, consider $100 as one value point. Go and enter 2.5 value points, instead of 0.1 hours, into your time-tracking and reporting program. The software doesn't know the difference between value points and hours — it will show a total of $250 (2.5 value points x $100 per point).

It's easy to use this method — you can still use the same time-tracking and reporting software. You must not, however, have committed to billing your client strictly by the hour. If you have done so, you will be stuck billing only $10 in the above example.

Whatever you do, spend time thinking about how you bill each and every client. Many people don't. They follow the old rules religiously. If "That's the way we've always done it" sounds familiar, you too are throwing away money.

TIME-TRACKING SECRETS

When you are just starting out, it's tempting to track your time manually — perhaps using random pieces of paper or even sticky notes to record your hours. If you do this, you might as well be putting a match to $100 bills. That's because it's easy to misplace these bits of paper. If you use this informal method, you may never recover full fees for your time and effort. I'll discuss time-tracking and recording software, but first, here are a few tips for recording all the hours you work.

Keep track during the day

No matter how you track your time, make sure you document it throughout your day. Do not leave the task until the end of the day or, heaven forbid, the end of the week. That's because you will probably forget at least some of the work that you did and which client you did it for.

I used to track time at the end of the day, but I often found that even though I was at my desk working hard for seven hours, I could never come up with seven hours worth of activities. That was money down the drain if it was time that could have been charged to clients.

Use increments of less than one hour

In the beginning you may work a full day on one task for one client. In that case, it's pretty easy to track time. You were at the client's office from 9:00 a.m. to 5:00 p.m. with an hour for lunch. That's seven hours on one task.

Once your client base grows, however, you should consider tracking time in increments of less than an hour. This is because you may deal with different projects for different clients every day. You'll find that they don't fit nicely into easily documented chunks of time. I often sit down to review one client file, only to be sidetracked by a phone call from another client. Then I find myself spending some time with another after I've checked my email. Once I started to track all my time, I quickly discovered exactly where it was going.

Lawyers are experts at this — they seem to bill for every little thing and often get down to six-minute increments. Why six? Because six minutes is one-tenth of an hour and is easy to track. Try 15 minutes if six seems too small, but be as fair and honest as you can.

Track chargeable and nonchargeable time

If you are truly serious about growing your business, you should track the time you can't charge to clients as well as the time you can. It forces you to spend time on the all-important tasks of running and growing your business.

For example, say selling and marketing don't come naturally to you, as is the case with me. I set a monthly target for the number of hours I'll spend on this. If I have not met the target by the end of the month, I will take steps to improve the next month.

The same goes for finance and administration. Consider how long this should take each month, and set a target for the number of hours you'll devote to it.

The advantage of planning for, and tracking the time you spend on, nonchargeable tasks is that it legitimizes the activity. You'll probably worry less about spending time on the work you don't get paid for if you prioritize it like this.

The other advantage is that it will show you where your time is going. You need to know this in order to make improvements in how you manage your time. Take email, for example. I used to check email several times every day. I then found out that I was wasting a lot of time I could have been spending on more important activities.

I now only check email when it is convenient, usually only once or twice a day. I also figured out how to use the "Blocked Senders List" in Microsoft Outlook to automatically send spam to my junk folder. There was one weekend recently where I didn't check my email, and I was out of the office on Monday. When I went online again on Tuesday, there were 469 messages: 389 of them were from blocked senders, but 80 still got into my in-box. Exactly how many of them were "real" emails? Four.

I also still had to search through my junk folder, as a few real emails had ended up there. I had to find a better solution. Did I spend hours browsing the Internet for an answer? No. I did what I usually do: I called an expert. In this case it was my web designers, Glen and Kelly Patchet of GK Media. Glen pointed me to www.qurb.com. I purchased their Anti-Spam product for about $30. It is excellent — now I rarely get junk in my in-box or find email misdirected to the junk folder.

TIME-TRACKING AND REPORTING SOFTWARE

In order to keep track of your hours, you need time-tracking and reporting (or billing) software. It resides on your computer and should accept time data either directly or from your handheld device.

There is no excuse not to use time-tracking and reporting software, with it being so affordable. Heck, there is even good software for this available for free on the Web. I just punched "time tracking software" into Google and got 134 million hits. You've got a lot of choices.

What to look for

Because there are so many choices, it is not always easy to select the right software for your needs. You should make sure it meets the following criteria:

- *Works on your handheld device.* There will be times you need to track your hours when you are not at your computer. If you always carry your handheld, you are more likely to record that time. If you have to wait until you get to your computer, you'll find time slipping through the cracks.

- *Room to enter activity details.* One of the freeware programs I looked at had sections for client, task, and activity, but no place to enter specific details about the activity. That's a major problem. Which of the following do you think a client would be more willing to pay extra for: "Project X — 1 hour" or "Project X — 20 minute conversation with Max Smith (federal government) regarding export rules; 40 minutes research regarding overseas jurisdiction import laws"? The more details you have, the easier it will be to justify your invoice when it comes time to bill.

- *Support staff available if needed.* This is imperative. It's worth choosing a reputable program that has the resources to back it up.

The quest for five-star time-tracking and reporting software

I used to use an old DOS-based program that performed the functions I needed but was inflexible and difficult to customize. It had the following problems:

- It did not allow me to import data. If I recorded my activities using the Microsoft Outlook calendar, I then had to manually enter each one into the time-tracking program.

- I had to do a monthly and year-end "close" and couldn't access data in prior months or years after they were closed.

- Setting up different projects for different clients was cumbersome.

- I could not add new projects on the fly. I had to go to the "clients" section each time.

- Bulky formulas were needed to customize reports for things like nonchargeable time.

- I had to manually enter client invoices each month in order to calculate any write-ups or write-downs for each client.

I continued to use the old DOS-based program for many years because I knew it would take time to research and find a replacement and then transfer all my information to it. With a busy schedule and clients to deal with, it was hard to find the necessary time, and, after all, the existing program could still do the job.

I finally became convinced that there had to be a better, more efficient program that would reduce the amount of time I was spending entering and analyzing time values and client write-ups and write-downs.

The process of finding a new program didn't take as long as I'd expected. I began by downloading a few freeware programs from the Web. In most cases they were good programs — I'm often surprised at the great software you can get for free these days. There were, however, a couple of major problems with the time-tracking and billing freeware:

- *Lack of support.* The people who develop the programs usually do it on the side and have other jobs that keep them busy. You can't expect them to drop everything and respond to your request for assistance in learning how to use their program or to fix any bugs or make other improvements to the software.

- *Lack of reporting function.* Creating summaries and reports required other software, which I usually didn't have. Some programs didn't even allow me to export the data to such software. This is a major problem. Others did allow an export, but produced only a rudimentary "CSV" (comma-separated values) text file.

- *Time versus dollars.* Many of the programs did not multiply the time by an hourly rate, presumably leaving it up to another program to perform this function.

The key to effective invoicing is in the analysis of the time reports. You could spend hours designing your own spreadsheet or database to track and analyze your time entries, but why bother? As I discovered, there are many inexpensive programs available that will do this for you.

Why I chose BillQuick

I had come to the conclusion that freeware was not going to provide the answer, and I shifted my focus to what programs were available for sale. The first place I looked was the website of the DOS program I had been using. The software company had improved the program significantly from the old version I was using, but it was geared to larger companies and was therefore expensive.

Ironically, that site directed me to another site, www.cpa technologyadvisor.com, which had awarded the DOS program 4.5 out of 5 stars. *CPA Technology Advisor* is a great site; it's aimed at accountants but contains a lot of reports and articles that are useful to the general reader. And it was at this site that I learned about BillQuick (www.billquick.com). *CPA Technology Advisor* had given it five out of five stars. I soon found out why.

First of all, anyone can download a free version of the program called BillQuick Lite. This is nearly identical to the full program, but it lacks a few features, such as the ability to import data from sources such as PDA devices. I downloaded the basic program for a 30-day free trial and then bought it for a few hundred dollars because I ended up needing the additional features.

The other remarkable thing about this company (no, I am not affiliated with it in any way) is that it provides support to everyone who uses the product, even if all they have is the 30-day evaluation copy. This was important to me. I wanted to make sure I could enter time entries on my Palm Treo 600 and synchronize the data with the program on my notebook (a Dell Inspiron 600m).

When I downloaded the Palm add-on, I somehow couldn't make it work. The Palm expert at BillQuick talked me through the problem and spent almost half an hour as I tested the synchronization feature until it worked. He then proceeded to show me around the main features of the software. This was before I even bought the program. If only more companies provided service like this.

I have found that I particularly like the following features:

- *The timer.* All I do is click on the clock icon and select the engagement (or project) that I am going to work on, and the program begins timing the activity. When I have finished the activity, I click on "Log" and the time is automatically entered in my time sheet.

- *The reports.* There are over 350 standard, ready-to-use report templates in the following categories:

Activity

Aging

Analysis

Billing

Client

Company

Employee

Engagement

Payments

The reports I use most frequently are "Work in Progress" and "Write Up/Write Down by Project."

"Work in Progress (Details)" lists the employee ID, description of his or her activity, the number of billable hours, and the cost and billable amount of this activity. It then calculates the total billable amount for the entire project, including the expenses you would charge to the client. You can filter by date, project, client, or employee and can choose active or inactive projects, billable or nonbillable time, and billed or unbilled projects. Figure 6 shows what the report looks like.

FIGURE 6
BILLQUICK WORK IN PROGRESS REPORT

XYZ Consulting Corporation

12345 This Street
Anytown, CA 00000
Tel: (310) 555-1212 Fax: (310) 555-2121
admin@xyzconsulting.com
www.xyz.com

| | Work in Progress (Details) |

Project ID: 04-098-AO:
Proj Name: All Over 2.0 Upgrade
Contract Amount: $11,500.00
Contract Type: Hourly Not to Exceed
Printed on: 4/12/2005

Date	Employee ID	Description	B-Hrs	Cost	Bill Amt
Services:					
3/10/2005	CJ	BLUE PRINTING	8.00	$280.00	$1,200.00
3/11/2005	CJ	BUILDING DEPARTMENT LIAISON	9.00	$315.00	$1,350.00
3/14/2005	CJ	CLASS/SEMINAR/EDUCATION	8.00	$280.00	$1,200.00
3/14/2005	CJ	CONSTRUCTION INSPECTION	9.00	$315.00	$1,350.00
3/16/2005	JA	BLUE PRINTING	8.00	$172.00	$480.00
3/17/2005	JA	DESIGN CALCULATIONS	9.00	$193.50	$540.00
3/18/2005	JA	ELECTRICAL PLANS	8.00	$172.00	$480.00
4/1/2005	RC	GEOTECHNICAL COORDINATION	8.00	$268.00	$880.00
4/4/2005	MK	BID PACKAGES	8.00	$220.00	$760.00
4/5/2005	MK	BID PACKAGES	8.00	$220.00	$760.00
4/6/2005	MK	BID PACKAGES	9.00	$247.50	$855.00
4/7/2005	MK	BID PACKAGES	8.00	$220.00	$760.00
		Total of Services for Project ID: 04-098-AO:	**100.00**	**$2,903.00**	**$10,615.00**
Expenses:					
4/1/2005	CJ	MILEAGE	25.00	$12.50	$13.75
4/4/2005	WB	SPECIAL DELIVERY/COURIER	1.00	$35.95	$39.55
4/7/2005	BD	COPY SERVICES	30.00	$9.00	$9.90
4/8/2005	CJ	MILEAGE	25.00	$12.50	$13.75
		Total Expenses for Project ID: 04-098-AO:	**81.00**	**$69.95**	**$76.95**
		Grand Total:		**$2,972.95**	**$10,691.95**

Figure 6, BillQuick Standard Report, copyright ©2005 is used by permission of BQE Software, Inc.

In this example you can see the total hours on the project (100), the total cost of the employees ($2,903), and the total billable amount ($10,615). Since the total contract amount (indicated above the breakdown) is $11,500, it means the project should be close to completion.

After you have generated your invoices (you can use the program to do so), you can instantly produce a report that lists all write-ups or write-downs on any or all projects. You can filter this report just as you can the work-in-progress report. Figure 7 shows a sample.

FIGURE 7
BILLQUICK WRITE UP/WRITE DOWN REPORT

XYZ Consulting Corporation
12345 This Street
Anytown, CA 00000
Tel: (310) 555-1212 Fax: (310) 555-2121
admin@xyzconsulting.com
www.xyz.com

Write Up/Write Down By Project

Printed on: 4/12/2005

Page 1 of 1

Employee Fee Analysis by Project

Project ID: 09-573:TECH: Project Name: Party Planners, Inc. Technical Support

Inv Num: 1119 Inv Date: 3/14/2005 Std Amt: $1,242.00 Act Amt: $1,600.00 Wu/Wd Amt: $358.00 Wu/Wd %: 29%

Employee ID	Employee Name	Hours	Std Amt	Std Rate	Act Amt	Act Rate	Wu/Wd %
AM	Allen Marcello	8.00	$160.00	$20.00	$206.12	$25.76	
AT&T	John Ramsey	8.00	$802.00	$100.25	$1,033.17	$129.15	
BD	Bob Duncan	4.00	$280.00	$70.00	$360.71	$90.18	
	Invoice Average:		$414.00	$62.10	$533.33	$80.00	

Inv Num: 1120 Inv Date: 3/21/2005 Std Amt: $1,380.00 Act Amt: $1,350.00 Wu/Wd Amt: ($30.00) Wu/Wd %: (2%)

Employee ID	Employee Name	Hours	Std Amt	Std Rate	Act Amt	Act Rate	Wu/Wd %
AM	Allen Marcello	8.00	$160.00	$20.00	$156.52	$19.57	
CJ	Curtis James	4.00	$600.00	$150.00	$586.96	$146.74	
JA	Jennifer Arlington	4.00	$240.00	$60.00	$234.78	$58.70	
MK	Mark Kerns	4.00	$380.00	$95.00	$371.74	$92.93	
	Invoice Average:		$345.00	$69.00	$337.50	$67.50	

	Project Average:			$65.55		$73.75	
	Project Total:	40.00	$2,622.00		$2,950.00		12.51%

Figure 7, BillQuick Standard Report, copyright ©2005 is used by permission of BQE Software, Inc.

This example shows two invoices for Project ID 09-573:TECH. Invoice number 1119 was for $1,600 (the actual amount) but the time value (the standard amount) only came to $1,242. The write-up is the difference between these amounts, $358, which is 29 percent of the time value.

Invoice 1120, on the other hand, was for $1,350, but the time value came to $1,380. The report shows the resulting write-down of $30, 2 percent of the time value.

This particular program has given me tools to optimize my billings. I wish I had discovered it sooner. I no longer have to enter time entries twice, and I am much less likely to let time, and therefore money, slip through the cracks.

If you charge for services rather products, your time is your most valuable asset. It's a limited asset. There are only so many hours in a day, week, or year. If you don't track it, you won't be able to determine where you are spending it, and you won't be able to make conscious decisions about how to use it more effectively. You'll also be throwing time away because you won't be able to bill what you don't track.

Start your business on the right foot — take the time to select the best time-tracking and reporting software and use it religiously.

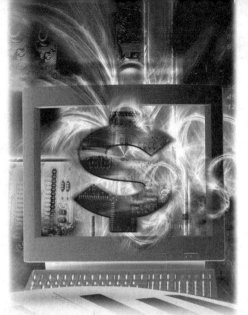

10

INTEGRATE YOUR LIFE
WITH YOUR BUSINESS

When I went off to university in 1977, I didn't have a clue what I wanted to do with my life. Since I was pretty good at math and science, engineering seemed like a logical choice, so that's what I went to study. I didn't enjoy it much, though, so after one term I switched to the faculty of science and earned a bachelor of science degree with a minor in business. This allowed me to get some business training, which I had a hunch would come in handy some day.

After graduating, I still didn't have any idea what I wanted to do with my life. I had always enjoyed photography as a hobby, so I tried a stint as a photographer. Taking family portraits at the back of a department store in a strip mall didn't work out, however. I remember feeling pretty lost and depressed.

It was at this point that I fell into accounting. It was a profession my dad, Peter, had always enjoyed, and it had provided well for our family. Interestingly, I didn't get my first accounting job by sending out thousands of résumés and attending numerous interviews. I got in through the back door. Ernst & Young (E&Y) was the auditor of the company my dad worked for. He got me in at the end of September 1981, after all the hiring for the year had been done, by making a call to see if there were any openings. Two recent hires had just quit so they took me on.

That was the most important event in my career. The firm had excellent people and superb training programs, and its philosophy was to always do things right, even if it took longer. E&Y was also interested in hiring a range of people with varying backgrounds. I didn't have much training in accounting when I started, and I vividly remember that in my first few weeks I was able to use work time to study accounting. At one point I went to my manager, a man named Dean Turner, and asked what "GL" stood for. (When you study accounting, you'll find out it means "general ledger," which is one of the most basic accounting terms there is.) Dean patiently explained the term. Thinking back on it, I often wonder what would have happened to me if my first boss had been one of the people I worked for after I left E&Y. I can think of two or three who would have destroyed me. I would have been laughed out onto the street and not be given a second thought. I am forever grateful Dean was my first boss.

I also remember my first partner, Colin Graham. He was one of the nicest, most intelligent people I have ever met in my life. Every year he would give his secretary a birthday present and make sure it was accompanied by a birthday card — always a Peanuts cartoon because that was what she liked. His example still inspires me today.

After I left E&Y, I spent several years working for others and then I ventured out on my own. Things got tougher, but as they say, what doesn't kill you makes you stronger. Along the way I've picked up many tips that affect the way I do business today. Interestingly, I have found that many of the tips that work for my business also work in my personal life. That is why I call them *Life Tips*. Try them out and see if they work for you.

LIFE TIP 1 — DO WHAT YOU DON'T WANT TO DO FIRST

I used to keep a to-do list that always had a dozen things on it. The problem was that I'd usually get to numbers one, two, and possibly three, but items four through twelve never seemed to get done, no matter how hard I tried.

I noticed that it was always the things I enjoyed doing that ended up getting done. I'd inevitably put those things first on the list. Now, maybe I'm a little weird, but I actually enjoy administrative tasks such as paying bills and doing my own bookkeeping. Marketing, on the other hand, did not come naturally to me, so I put it off until later. Guess what: I never used to get around to spending any time on marketing.

The same applies in my personal life. I am not a big fan of household chores, like gardening, for example. The thought of getting dirty pulling weeds for several hours doesn't turn my crank. However, it, like marketing, needs to be done.

Whether it's for my business or personal life, I now put the task that I don't like to do — important but not enjoyable to me — first on the list. And I do it first! You'll probably find, as I still do, that this is difficult. Just getting started is the hardest part, but once you start you may find that most things are not as difficult or unpleasant as you had imagined.

If you stick to this principle, you'll be rewarded by a feeling of accomplishment and with actually getting the task done. And don't worry. You'll always have time for the tasks you like to do.

LIFE TIP 2 — YOU GET WHAT YOU EXPECT

The simple truth is that if you don't expect to get something, chances are you won't get it. I wish I had learned this earlier in my life, before I turned 40. It certainly would have helped when I was a teen — I probably would have had more dates during those difficult years.

I now know why the jocks got all the dates. They had the self-confidence to *expect* that the answer would be yes. I, on the other hand, did not have any self-confidence. Whenever I did get the nerve to ask someone on a date, I was just *hoping* that she would say yes.

People can easily sense the difference. Think back to your youth. When someone asking you out practically begged you to say yes, were you interested? Or were you more interested in the person who didn't even seem to know you existed?

I think the same applies to sports. As I write this, the French Open is taking place. I read a quote by two-time major tournament winner Lleyton Hewitt, who had just lost a match to Rafael Nadal. Hewitt commented that Nadal was "very much like [Roger] Federer, winning so many matches that it's sort of second nature for him. They get down break point, and they expect to get out of it."

And the same basic principle applies to business. When you start out and are scrounging for any business you can get, clients can feel your desperation. This puts them in a position of power over you, from which they negotiate a price below what you are worth.

Unfortunately, I don't have a quick fix for this problem. Naturally confident, outgoing people have a great edge here. They intrinsically act as if they expect to get that new client. I am far from a naturally confident person, but I find the best way to overcome this problem is to learn as much as I can and then become as proficient as possible at my chosen craft. This gives me the confidence to ask for what I am worth — and to walk away if I don't get it.

Coincidentally, you will probably find that your business grows as your confidence grows. The ideal objective is to get so good at what you do that you have a stable of ideal clients who value your services and pay you a good fee for doing what you love to do. This is the apex of your business. At this point you will have people coming to you through referrals, asking to be your client or customer, and you will be able to turn away nonideal business. You will also have the ultimate bargaining power when you are setting fees. If a client balks at paying what you think you're worth, you won't do business together.

LIFE TIP 3 — BALANCE IS THE KEY

As we saw in the section of Chapter 3 on establishing a niche, putting all your eggs in one basket is risky. If all you do is work, you are likely to end up burned-out, with few friends. The key to a healthy business and a healthy life is to balance work and play. Pay attention to your business but also to your friends and family. Take time off and get away from work. You'll find that this is also the best way to attract good customers and clients — they like to deal with people who are interesting and well rounded. Workaholics don't tend to make good "finders." How can you attract business if you're always slaving away in the office?

This also brings up the issue of physical fitness. You must work at keeping your body fit as well as your mind. All it takes is 20 minutes of exercise three times a week. That's 1 hour out of 168 in a week. You don't have to go to a fancy gym with saunas, whirlpools, the latest weight machines, and computerized treadmills. What about a brisk walk or jog starting at your front door? Or maybe a bike ride, which is much easier on the knees? My dad's preference was squash. When he worked, he used to play at the local club at least three times a week. After the game, he'd sit in the lounge over a beer (or two) with his buddies. He often said that after a hard day of difficult decisions, any outstanding problems and issues would magically disappear for a few hours during and after his games. That allowed him to get a good night's sleep and wake up with the resulting fresh frame of mind needed to face the day.

What about you — do you get regular exercise? If you. do, you'll be much better off in business and in life.

LIFE TIP 4 — PLAN ON A WEEKLY, NOT A DAILY, BASIS

I discovered this tip, to plan your week rather than your day, in one of the best books I have ever read, *The 7 Habits of Highly Effective People*, by Stephen R. Covey (Simon & Schuster, 2004).

Spreading the items over a full five-day week, instead of trying to fit them all in one day, is tremendously freeing. It allows you to put most of the items out of mind and focus on fewer things at a time. In fact, it's best to focus on just one single thing at any one time. You'll find it incredibly empowering.

When you have given yourself too many things to do in one day, it's common to get sidetracked. Worrying wastes a lot of energy and time and significantly reduces the effort that is being expended on the current task. As a result, most tasks take longer to do and don't get done well if they're done at all. In some cases, completed tasks have to be done over again because they were done so poorly the first time. Personally, I have adopted the philosophy that it's better to get fewer tasks done well than to get more done poorly.

LIFE TIP 5 — BE FLEXIBLE WITH YOUR TIME *

In an attempt to get myself to focus on selling and marketing, I once tried to set aside Friday afternoons just for marketing activities. Inevitably, I'd get a phone call, or a client would need to meet, or a Monday deadline would get in the way. It just didn't work.

I agree with Benjamin Franklin on this one. In his autobiography he says he tried optimizing his time by breaking each day into hourly blocks dedicated to particular tasks. His conclusion? It doesn't work. When I read that, I gave up on my own attempts to stringently allocate my time.

That's not to say you should be casual with your time. It means you have to accept that things won't always go the way you want them to go. Focus on key activities, but be prepared for things to happen where you end up doing something else.

Be careful with this one, however. It's easy to get drawn away from important tasks by unimportant ones. The telephone is often a problem here. I used to answer my phone whenever it rang. On a busy day it would interrupt me several times. On exceptionally busy days, a task that I should have finished by lunch would still be in the early stages at the end of the day. I now screen all calls to my business line. I don't answer my cell phone, but let it take messages. When I write, I leave my office downtown and work in my home office (as I am doing at this moment). I have found this is the only way to ensure important tasks get done. Remember that the phone is there for your convenience, not someone else's.

LIFE TIP 6 — DON'T BE AFRAID TO ASK A STUPID QUESTION

When I was in school, I hardly ever raised my hand to ask a question in class. I was too scared that I would say something silly and end up embarrassed. I am sure that stunted my learning and my ability to get along with people.

As I've gotten older, I have found that asking simple questions is the best thing you can do. It's actually a good way to make new friends and clients. If you are interested enough in what people might have to say, you'll often be amazed at what they tell you and what connections you can make.

I am also not afraid to let people know when I don't have a clue what they are talking about. The results are fascinating. Often, when I ask people to explain what they mean in plain English, they can't do it. That usually means they don't understand what they are saying either. I don't do this to embarrass them; I do it because I am genuinely interested in understanding what it is they are trying to tell me.

This strategy is also useful if you are trying to find out if someone is telling you the truth. Don't fool yourself into thinking you can tell when someone is lying to you — you can't. This was pointed out to me after I did a personality test. I had answered about 100 multiple-choice questions, and the testers concluded that I was pretty normal and that like most people I couldn't tell whether someone was lying to me. Ever since that test, I assess what people say to me with a dose of skepticism. That was a valuable lesson for me early in my life, and I'm sure it has helped me avoid some disastrous experiences.

In your life, you are likely to meet people who know exactly what they are talking about but choose to tell you only what they think you want to hear or what they want you to know. (Salespeople sometimes fall into this category.) They may even be twisting the truth. If you simply believe what people tell you and, as a result, buy a product or service you don't quite understand, you'll often end up the loser if things go wrong.

On a more positive note, asking simple questions is an effective way to make new friends. Just ask potential friends or clients about something they are interested in and let them talk. People love to talk if you let them. This can be both good and bad. On the good side, you'll get to know many people who are humble, thoughtful, and considerate — the kind of friends you'd like for life. They'll often turn things around and ask you about your life and interests, and they'll actually listen.

On the bad side, you'll probably end up talking to some of the most overbearing jerks imaginable. For many years I have been fascinated by this latter category. These people love to talk about themselves — how much they earn, how great their jobs are, how wonderful their kids are, the great things they have achieved. I always wonder what they are trying to prove. In most cases you'll find these people make bad friends, bad clients, and bad business partners. Can you imagine dealing with someone like this day after day?

If you are trying to make friends and clients, be a listener and a questioner, not a lecturer.

LIFE TIP 7 — STAY AWAY FROM THOSE WHO SAY YOU CAN'T DO IT

Whether you succeed or not will depend to a large degree on how motivated you are. It seems many people in the world today are not all that motivated. These people see the negative in almost everything — they see the glass as half empty.

These are not the kinds of people you want to discuss your small-business dream with. If you can, avoid them altogether.

There is a fine line here. I am not saying that you should avoid people who might have some constructive criticism for you. In fact, I encourage you to speak with as many people as you can about your business, especially if you already know people in your chosen industry. Just stay away from those who belittle your small-business dream.

Becoming and staying motivated is a huge issue. There will be days when you don't even feel like rolling out of bed. If you are just starting a business, or if you are working at someone else's business as you learn your craft, try to find a mentor. A mentor is someone who has experience in your field, will take the time to show you the ropes, and possibly introduce you to people who will also help you progress.

If you can't find such a role model, seek support by reading books. One book I have found extremely motivating is *Awaken the Giant Within: How to Take Immediate Control of Your Mental, Emotional, Physical and Financial Destiny!*, by Anthony Robbins (Free Press, 1992). Yes, I know what many of you might think of Anthony Robbins. I thought the same thing before I actually read the book. No matter how you view Robbins, however, he is a master at motivating people to set high goals and take steps to reach them. *Awaken the Giant Within* gave me the self-confidence and motivation to start writing on my own, without worrying about what people thought. You may not agree with all his ideas, but you can't lose by reading his book.

LIFE TIP 8 — DON'T BE AFRAID OF YOUR COMPETITION

Remember not to ignore your competition. Some of my best sources of client referrals have been other accountants. Many of them specialize in different areas than I do, and they may be unable to help a client who needs the services I can offer. They refer clients to me, and I also refer clients to them when it makes sense.

Other people in your field know what you do. You don't need to explain to them the basic services you offer. This is important if your business is a bit specialized. If you rely on referral sources such as friends and family, who do not know exactly what it is that you do, it will be impossible for them to identify people and situations where your services are needed.

Your competitor may even become a future business partner. Or perhaps he or she will decide to leave the business and will want someone to take over from them. You just never know.

Even if you don't end up getting to know your competition, you can learn a lot about them. The Internet makes this easy. Do a Google search to find out what products and services other local businesses offer and how they do their marketing. Even pricing information is widely available.

LIFE TIP 9 — LEAVE LOTS OF TIME FOR COMPLETING EACH TASK

I used to be a procrastinator. I'd put off doing tasks fearing they would take a long time. When I did something, I'd try to complete the job in as short a period as possible. This was endlessly frustrating because when I did get around to doing things, I always proved myself right — "See, this is taking too long."

Now I leave more than enough time to do each task. This makes even mundane tasks more enjoyable. Another benefit is that it gets you focused on the task. As I mentioned in Life Tip 4, if you try to fit 12 tasks into one day, you'll spend a lot of time thinking about all the tasks left to do. This means you do a poor job on the task you're doing and you get stressed out over those that aren't being done.

The other advantage to leaving lots of time to complete a task is that you'll be less rushed and less likely to be late for the next thing. I used to try to do as much as I could in as little time before moving on to the next task. But I *would* go overtime on one task and be late for the next, which is a problem that snowballs over the course of the day. Don't plan to do too much — leave enough time so your life does not become one big race to the finish line.

LIFE TIP 10 — DON'T WAIT FOR EVERYTHING TO BE PERFECT

Years ago, I was never happy until everything was just right in my life — personal relationships all healthy, business going well, good cash flow, time for my hobbies, outstanding business issues nicely tied up, etc. Guess what. I wasn't happy very often.

Now I make sure I enjoy the moment whenever I can. That may be on a Monday afternoon, when I play hooky to go watch a movie after completing a writing assignment. Or it could be on a Thursday, when I take time off work to go to a theme park with my daughter, even though I have a client deadline on Friday.

I have found this is an important principle for people who deal with computers. I used to get frustrated when my computer wasn't working just perfectly. I would spend hours trying to get it tuned just right. Nine times out of ten, it never got there. Now I just accept that it won't ever be perfect. Almost perfect is all I expect.

▣   ▣   ▣

There you have it — ten tips I have used to integrate my business and personal life and to improve both. You don't have to follow them all. Feel free to develop your own philosophy. Your business and your life will be more enjoyable if you do.

11

THE MILLIONAIRE DREAM: I'LL SELL IT AND GET RICH!

One of the significant advantages that a small-business owner has over people who slave away at jobs their entire lives is that the owner is building something with potentially great value — a business. Don't fool yourself, though. Most small businesses will never be sold because they don't have value to anyone else. Let's explore why.

BUSINESS VALUATION METHODS

Basically, your business is worth what an independent, objective party would pay for it. Unfortunately, there are no hard-and-fast rules for determining what that amount is, but it usually comes down to the bottom line — how much profit does the business make? Think about it. If your business doesn't make any profit, why would anyone buy it when they could invest in a savings account, make a small return, and be guaranteed their money back?

That's what you are competing against. If you are going to sell your business, it will have to have value to the person buying it. Looking back, it's easy to see that this was one of the main problems with the dot-com boom and bust. People were investing money in companies that were losing money. In fact, many of the companies did not have any idea where the *sales* were going to come from, let alone how they would make a profit. It didn't make sense then and it still doesn't today.

There are three basic ways that a business can be valued:

- Profit multiple

- Book value

- Service business

We'll look at each of these in turn.

Business valuation method 1: Profit multiple

There are times when you don't value a business based on its profits — for example, if your business has a unique product or process that potential purchasers think they can use to grow the business more effectively — but in most cases the measure of a business's value is the amount of profit it has made in the past and expects to make in the future.

This is the preferred method for valuing manufacturing and some retail companies. Profit is often defined as earnings before interest and taxes (EBIT). The value of the company is calculated by multiplying the EBIT by something we call a "multiple." This is usually the number of years it would take to recover the cost of buying the company.

(This is the same concept as the Price/Earnings [P/E] ratio used on public companies. This method involves dividing the company's current share price [P] by its earnings per share [E] to obtain a multiple. A P/E ratio of less than ten is often considered reasonable. Sometimes it gets crazy — a ratio of 100 or more means it would take about 100 years of earnings to equal the current share price. That would probably not be a good time to invest.)

This method is most suitable for companies that have an established earnings record. Say, for example, that a company has consistently showed EBIT of $20,000 per year for the last five years and is expected to produce the same amount of profit over the next five years. An investor willing to pay $100,000 for this company would recover the cost of the company in five years. The multiple in this case is five (five years x $20,000 EBIT per year = $100,000). Another way of looking at this is that the investor is assuming a 20 percent annual rate of return on the investment.

That's a good rate of return, but there is always an element of risk — no one knows what the future will hold. Will the business continue to be as profitable with new owners? The business may suffer, and profits may decline. The investor would then have paid too much. Maybe the new owners can *improve* the bottom line and do better than a 20 percent annual return. There's risk but there's also the possibility of reward.

Note that it is often difficult to determine the average earnings figure. No business makes the exact same profit several years in a row. If the business's profit ranged from $10,000 to $80,000 over the last five years, it becomes more difficult to determine an EBIT dollar figure.

Often adjustments must also be made to the reported earnings to account for unusual items such as bonuses paid to the owner, excessive salaries paid to the owner's children, above-market rents paid to related companies, and the costs of automobiles that are used for personal as well as business purposes. Discounting these items allows potential investors to get a more accurate idea of the actual earnings they are likely to make in the future when such costs are eliminated.

The multiple is another wildcard. Generally, the more stable the business is, the greater the multiple. If you are sure a business will be around for the next ten years and will continue to generate similar profits as in the past, a multiple of ten may be reasonable. If, however, due to changing market conditions or technology, there is a risk the business will not make it through the next three years, the multiple would be less — maybe as small as three.

If you are selling a corporation, you have to decide whether to sell shares or assets. There are legal implications to this decision. For instance, if you sell shares, the buyer acquires all the assets as well as the business's liabilities and commitments, whether they are disclosed or not. This increases the risk to buyers. If you just sell the assets, the buyer is not responsible for the liabilities or commitments. You should definitely seek the advice of a lawyer in this case.

Taxation also plays a major role in the decision. Basically, a seller is better off, taxwise, selling shares because of the favorable treatment of capital gains, and a buyer is better off acquiring only the assets because they can be written off or expensed against the income of the business. Seek professional tax advice from an accountant before selling a business.

If you are serious about finding out what your business is or will be worth, it's best not to rely on simple rules of thumb that I have touched on. Once again, get a professional — a business valuator (which I am not) will help you get it done right.

Business valuation method 2: Book value

This method focuses on the balance sheet rather than the income statement of a business. It is commonly used for non-service businesses and as a test check for businesses valued using the profit multiple method. The book value method is most useful in cases where the business is losing money — it doesn't make much sense to multiply a negative earnings number and get a negative value.

Using this method, you value the assets (i.e., accounts receivable, office furniture and equipment, and inventory) and subtract the liabilities (i.e., accounts payable, bank loans, and taxes owing). The difference between the assets and the liabilities is the book value.

Often adjustments are made to the asset values. For example, accounts receivables that are not collectible might be taken out of the equation, or the value of obsolete inventory would be reduced, or "written down." On the other hand, buildings or land may be worth more than the historical cost on financial statements, so their value would be "written up."

The buyer may also be willing to pay a premium over the book value, perhaps because the company has a great relationship with its customers, and the new owner is confident that he or she can increase sales and profits.

Business valuation method 3: Service business

The value of a service business lies in its employees and its customers. Such a business usually doesn't have many hard assets, such as inventory or equipment, so the book value method is not usually applicable. A service business also doesn't usually have a steady earnings stream. Its earning are contingent on who the clients are, what services they need, and the staff's ability to provide them. As a result, service businesses are often valued based on their client billings.

In the accounting industry, for example, a buyer often starts by assuming that 100 percent of client billings paid over a number of years will continue indefinitely. The question a buyer has to ask is: Are those billings actually repeatable?

Usually the clients have a strong relationship with the original owner. The clients are not required to stay with the firm after that owner sells his or her practice. In many cases, the clients are about the same age as the owner. This leads to the issue of retirement. Often when the owner wants to sell his or her practice to retire, the clients are also thinking of retiring. This means that when an owner leaves or retires, the buyer may not receive future work from clients who have been repeat customers in the past.

For these reasons, the value of a service business is often based on a percentage rather than a fixed amount and is spread over a number of years. For example, say Joe Seller has a client base with annual billings of $250,000. Jim Buyer wants to buy Joe's company and offers to pay 20 percent of the future annual billings over the next five years, to be paid to Joe at the end of each year.

Joe is 65, and so are many of his clients, so the billings for his clients decline over the next five years, as shown in Figure 8.

FIGURE 8
SALE PRICE BASED ON A PERCENTAGE OF FUTURE BILLINGS

Year	Gross billings	20% of billings
1	$230,000	$46,000
2	$210,000	$42,000
3	$190,000	$38,000
4	$170,000	$34,000
5	$150,000	$30,000
Total	$950,000	$190,000

Instead of paying $250,000 based on the current average billings, Jim only pays $190,000 in total. Furthermore, he benefits from spreading the payments over five years.

ARE YOU BUILDING IT TO SELL IT?

You don't necessarily have to think about selling your business from the day you start it, but you'd be wise to keep the issue in mind as the business grows. Even if you don't end up selling it, the process of improving it for sale will naturally result in a better business.

Make it work without you

Unless your business is like an accounting practice, where a new owner and staff can easily perform most of the basic functions that the old owner and staff did, it's worth thinking about how to set up your business so that it can operate efficiently without you. If you don't, the business will only have value if you are there every day. If your business grinds to a halt when you're not there, then you won't have much luck selling it unless you're part of the sale.

Some of the best advice comes from the E-Myth philosophy of Michael E. Gerber (www.e-myth.com). His theory is that most small-business owners are "technicians suffering from an entrepreneurial seizure." According to Gerber, because they know how to do the actual work of the business, they also believe they know everything about operating a profitable business. He says that most people don't own a true business, they own a job — working day in and day out *in* the business rather than *on* the business. Not many people will offer to buy your business if it is just a job in disguise.

Make it big enough

For the same reason, your business will also have to be big enough to attract buyers. You're unlikely to find someone who will pay you for a consulting business that has only one or two clients and grosses less than $90,000 per year. I am not belittling small consulting firms. This may be all you require to fulfill your needs. If you are trying to build a business that can be sold, however, you are playing a different game, as you'll see in the following example.

Stuart runs Business A. It's an engineering consulting firm that grosses $120,000 and nets Stuart $90,000 per year after expenses. Stuart is the only employee, and the company has two main clients. Stuart's life is pretty simple. He visits each client regularly, bills by the hour, and sends out two invoices each month. The invoices are paid within 20 days. Stuart does not plan to sell his business, as he knows this would be difficult.

Jim runs Business B, a residential kitchen renovation company that grossed $1 million last year and made a profit of $40,000. It has ten full-time employees and a $400,000 bank loan. Jim's pay last year was $90,000, and his life is always stressful. He is constantly looking for new jobs and developing extensive quotes to try and win them. The bank is frequently on his case and wants cash-flow projections monthly. He must keep an eye on his accounts receivable at all times, and he has had problems with customers refusing to pay due to disputes over extras that weren't included in the original quote.

Jim also has problems finding and retaining good employees, is often dealing with scheduling problems caused by customers who want things done immediately, and constantly worries that there will be a downturn in the economy that will reduce the demand for high-end kitchen renovations.

Because of the company's specialty, several larger companies are potentially interested in buying the business. But their interest comes with a catch — they want Jim to stay on for at least a few years because of his expertise and ability to produce accurate quotes.

Both Stuart and Jim take home the same salary — $90,000. Stuart's life is simple and flexible. Jim's is not, but he may be able to sell his business and pocket a six-figure amount. Who would you rather be? Or would you prefer to be somewhere between Stuart and Jim — creating a business that gives you a good income and has the potential to be sold, but that does not cause too much heart attack-inducing stress?

Take time for planning

How much time do most small-business owners spend thinking about how to make their business run without them? Maybe a few hours a week? An hour a month? Most of them don't devote much, if any, time to this vital issue. That's like taking a long car trip but not bothering to check whether any of the other passengers are licensed. If you stop driving, the trip ends. There has got to be a better way.

I have found that planning is an activity best done away from the office. If you are at your desk, there will always be many seemingly urgent things to distract you. That phone call, the fax that just came in, an employee's question about some time off, the mail, etc. Try getting away from things for a full day once in a while. This is tough to do in the beginning, especially if you are on your own. After all, if you are not there, you aren't making money. But, in the long run, doing this will make you money. If you ever want to sell your business, it must be able to make money without you grinding things out every day.

Why not try it this month? Set aside one day, take your accounting records for the last few years and the year-to-date as well as any notes you may have about your business operations, and do some analysis and brainstorming. Was last year profitable? What about this year so far? Which projects or products were the most profitable? Which jobs did you enjoy doing? Which ones did you do and which did other people do? Is there a certain niche your company has identified?

You may recognize that a task you have done a certain way for years is actually a waste of time and should be eliminated. You may identify a client who is difficult to deal with, pays late, and complains a lot, and decide to let him or her go.

If you are like me, you will find these days tremendously motivating and productive and will want to schedule more of them. If you don't set aside time for planning, you're missing the opportunity to increase the value of your business and the quality of your life.

12

COULD A FRANCHISE
BE FOR YOU?

Buying a franchise is one way to start your own business. You can choose from many different types ranging from coffee shops to lawn maintenance or home improvement companies. You can begin to sell goods or services that have immediate brand-name recognition and at the same time receive training and marketing support from experienced people in that industry.

While they are often more expensive than starting your own business from scratch, franchises statistically have a greater success rate because the product or service already has a proven track record. But beware. Choosing the wrong one could cost you thousands of dollars and ruin your dream of self-employment.

WHAT IS A FRANCHISE ANYWAY?

There is much confusion about what a franchise is exactly. When you buy a franchise, you are not buying a business. You are buying the right to sell particular products or services developed by someone else for a certain period of time — usually ranging from 10 to 20 years — in a particular area. There are often renewal options as well.

A franchise is actually a legal agreement between a seller (the franchisor) and a buyer (the franchisee) that requires the franchisee to pay various fees and royalties. For these fees, the franchisor grants the right to use the company name for a limited time and to use a given format or system developed to sell the goods or services. Franchisors generally provide ongoing support, including help with finding a location, management training, marketing, and dealing with staffing requirements.

Advantages of a franchise

There are many advantages to investing in an established franchise rather than starting on your own.

- *Proven products or services.* There is significantly reduced risk of the product or service not selling, and you can easily determine the success of the product or service ahead of time by studying existing franchises. (When you are starting your very own business the research is harder to do, and if you don't do enough you may learn too late that there is little demand for what you are selling.)

- *Proven systems.* The franchisor will usually have developed detailed policies and procedures on how to actually run the business. These systems run the gamut from operations (how and when to order more stock, how to make the product) to marketing (where and how to advertise, use of the logo or brand) and finance and administration (what accounting software to use, how to enter information, and what key reports to focus on to ensure the business is running well). These are usually documented in formal manuals, which make it easier for inexperienced entrepreneurs just starting out. These manuals are also useful for training new employees.

- *Training.* While a good manual is an excellent way to learn, there is nothing better than hands-on training from someone experienced in operating the specific business. Most franchisors offer this type of training to help franchisees set up, run, and grow their businesses. This is much easier, and often cheaper, than learning from your mistakes along the way.

- *Ongoing supervision and advice.* A good franchisor will be happy to provide advice and assistance about running the business to the franchisee. This is akin to having a valuable mentor by your side as you experience the pain and joys of growing a business. It is a huge advantage to be able to call someone who has "been there, done that" whenever you have a pressing issue or problem.

- *Ongoing product/service development.* As we discussed earlier in Chapter 3 on niches, any successful business must constantly work at developing new products and services to meet the future demands of customers and clients. With a good franchise operation, this will be done for you by the franchisor, which saves you a lot of time and effort.

- *Purchasing power.* With so many franchisees contributing funds, the successful franchisor is able to afford regional and even national marketing campaigns. Small businesses with only one or two locations can't afford to pay for this type of advertising. The larger volume of business also allows the franchisor to achieve economies of scale when it comes to purchasing supplies. For example, a pizza chain that uses 60,000 pounds of dough a year can buy it more cheaply than a shop that only uses 1,000 pounds a year.

- *Financing.* Many franchises have arrangements with financial institutions that make it easier for new franchisees to obtain financing. Bankers know about the business based on existing franchises — it's a proven commodity, and bankers like that the best.

Disadvantages of a franchise

Unfortunately, buying a franchise is by no means a guarantee of success. Be aware of the following disadvantages:

- *The cost.* Franchises can be expensive. There is the initial franchise fee, loan costs (if you have to borrow money to purchase the franchise), ongoing royalty fees (usually based on sales), as well as any start-up costs for items such as equipment, merchandise, and supplies. (See the next section for more details.)

- *Reduced flexibility.* The franchisor determines how you run the business. This includes deciding what products and services you can sell, how you can sell them, and for what price. You may also be limited in terms of where you can buy your products and services and even how you do your accounting. These strict guidelines mean that you become more of a manager than an entrepreneur. Again, this may be what you need, but if you wish to be truly free to pursue your own ideas, buying a franchise may not be for you.

- *Limited expansion opportunities.* Many successful franchisees own more than one franchise. This is a great way to become successful, but one potential drawback is that the franchisor determines whether and when you can buy additional locations. You are not in control of your own destiny.

- *Demanding work.* The franchisor will want you to be successful. If a franchisor has many successful franchisees, he or she collects more money from them and can sell even more franchises. To encourage a successful franchise, franchisors will likely require you to put in a lot of hours. For example, retail locations will have set hours of business — in some cases, seven days a week. Franchisors may also require you to set aside time to produce specialized management reports.

- *You could be stuck in a declining business.* What happens if you sign a legal agreement to operate a business for 15 years, but after two years there is a major decline in demand for the product or service? With a franchise, that's a real risk you take — you could be stuck with a lemon of a business with no exit strategy.

HOW MUCH IS A FRANCHISE WORTH?

The type of franchise you are interested in will have a significant impact on how much you will have to pay for it. There are two basic types:

- *Product/service and logo franchises.* The franchisee buys the right to distribute a product or offer a service using a brand name. Examples include auto dealerships and janitorial or maid services.

- *Business format franchises.* The franchisee buys the right to distribute a product or offer a service using a brand name, but he or she is also purchasing an entire business operation. Franchisors provide a lot more support, including operating procedures, marketing plans, quality control standards, and facility design. Examples include fast-food restaurants and hair salons. This type of franchise usually costs a lot more.

Most franchises of either type will also charge the following fees:

- *Initial franchise fee.* This up-front fee is often nonrefundable and can range from several thousand to several hundred thousand dollars. It is often payable when you sign the franchise agreement.

- *Opening fee.* You may be required to pay a "grand opening" fee to announce the opening of your location.

- *Royalty fees.* You will likely have to pay ongoing royalties based on a percentage of your gross income (sales). These fees are often calculated monthly or quarterly. Remember that what you make is your net income, which is gross income less any expenses of the business. You may have to make royalty payments even if you are losing money, and that can create a significant cash-flow problem. In addition, these fees are usually just for the right to use the franchisor's name, not for any support services the franchisor may provide, so you may have to continue paying the fees even if you no longer receive the support services.

- *Advertising fees.* Franchisors often require another fee based on a percentage of your sales to support their advertising efforts. Some of these funds may pay for national campaigns, and some may be directed at attracting more franchisees. You'll have little control over whether the money you send is used for advertising to customers and clients in your region.

- *Other costs.* You may have to pay for additional items such as employee training, operating licenses, insurance, and the interest costs on any loans you take out to buy and equip the business operation.

QUESTIONS TO ASK BEFORE YOU BUY

When you consider starting any business, it's important to do as much work as you can beforehand to make sure you are getting into something that will suit your skills and requirements. Franchising is no exception. In fact, it is probably even more essential that you do your homework before signing a franchise agreement because you are risking a potentially large amount of your own money and committing to something for a significant number of years. Ask yourself the following questions:

About the money:

- How much do you have to invest?

- If you need to borrow money, are you likely, given your credit rating, to be approved for a loan?

- How much business debt do you feel comfortable with?

- If the business does not work and you lose your investment, will you be able to recover financially?

- If you require a certain salary, can this franchise provide it?

- Will the franchise be a primary or secondary source of income?

About yourself:

- Are you sure that you enjoy this business enough to spend 15 or 20 years doing it?

- Do you have administrative skills such as computer skills?

- Does the franchise require technical knowledge and experience that will necessitate extensive training?

- Should you seek out partners with skills you don't have?

- How many hours a week are you willing to work?

- Is your family keen on the idea of you devoting your time to this venture?

- Do you like dealing with people? (You will be interacting with a lot of people, including customers, employees, the franchisor's staff, suppliers, and other franchisees.)

- Are you willing to follow strict guidelines or do you like to do your own thing?

About the franchise:

- Does it have a solid track record?

- Are existing franchisees generally happy with it?

WATCH OUT FOR SCAMS

Since franchising in general is perceived to be less risky than starting an independent business, it naturally attracts many budding entrepreneurs. Unfortunately, there are individuals who take advantage of these people's dreams of starting their own business and dupe them with schemes that are nothing short of fraud.

One of the most common scams involves a franchise offer that claims franchisees will earn inordinate amounts of money. It's hard to resist when the promise is thousands of dollars a week for little effort. Fortunately there are government and other agencies working hard to prevent this type of crime.

Just recently the United States government conducted "Project Biz Opp Flop," exposing promoters of illegal business opportunities. The Federal Trade Commission (FTC), the Department of Justice, the US Postal Inspection Service, and law-enforcement agencies from 14 states took action against more than 200 operations that had engaged in fraud and violated consumer protection laws. These frauds caused substantial consumer losses — tens of thousands of consumers lost more than $100 million.

Investigators identified these schemes by reviewing print, broadcast, and electronic media and contacting the promoters who plugged the business opportunities and their earnings potential. The investigators followed up with references provided by the promoters to substantiate the earnings claims. In many cases, these references turned out to be "ringers" — actors paid to pose as successful owner-operators.

Examples of franchise fraud

The following examples describe cases where the FTC alleges the promoters' statements about their opportunity were false or misleading:

- *Movie rentals.* An organization based in Hollywood, Florida, convinced people to buy its DVD-movie vending machines by promising significant earnings potential and assistance in finding locations. Customers were charged $28,000 to $37,500 for each machine and were told to expect to earn between $60,000 and $80,000 a year. The court-ordered receiver calculated that in less than one year consumers invested nearly $20 million.

- *Surplus goods.* An association based in Burbank, California, operating under several different names, offered work-at-home opportunities selling overstocked or discontinued merchandise. It promised franchisees that it would secure 200 customers, and it provided a list of references — allegedly successful, current brokers who had pursued this business opportunity — who they could call. The FTC said that individuals made initial payments of $4,000 to $7,950, which they lost.

- *Fridge magnets.* A company based in Mainesburg, Pennsylvania, offered a work-at-home opportunity involving the assembly of kitty-cat refrigerator magnets. The company promised up to $800 a week and $3,200 a month in revenue. Individuals paid $38 for registration and a starter kit, and $12 for an "inspection fee." According to the FTC, in most cases the assembly work was rejected for "quality" reasons. More than 30,000 people bought into the scam and lost their money.

How to spot a scam

Unfortunately, there is no website or organization that lists every business opportunity that is actually a scam. Your main source of protection is to educate yourself. Watch for the following danger signs:

- The business promises large profits with little work required. Watch for words like "fast cash," "minimal work," "no risk," and "work-at-home."

- Your contact at the business is unable to provide key statistics such as average sales, profits, and existing locations.

- Your contact is reluctant to identify key officers or principals. If he or she does give you a name, your first step should be to Google it.

- It sounds like the business is too good to be true.

- Your contact asks you to act immediately so you can get in on the ground floor. (Any legitimate business will expect you to take your time and do your research before committing to anything.)

- The company promises that the product or service is "easy to sell."

- The company has a name that sounds similar to a national reputable company but is not actually affiliated with that company.

Always check with the Better Business Bureau (www.bbb.org) in your area to check out any business opportunity before you sign anything.

In the United States, you should also check the FTC website (www.ftc.gov) for further information about avoiding scams and to find out about specific situations under investigation. The FTC files a complaint when it has reason to believe that the law has been violated. (The complaint does not mean that the defendant has actually violated the law. All cases are decided in a court of law.)

Don't leave it up to fate whether you lose your life savings or not.

THE FIVE MOST FREQUENTLY ASKED QUESTIONS ABOUT FRANCHISES

According to the FTC, the following are the five most frequently asked questions about franchise and business opportunities:

Where can I get a company's presale disclosure document?

In the United States, the FTC's Franchise Rule requires franchisors to provide a disclosure document or franchise-offering circular to prospective purchasers. Franchisors are not required to file these documents with the FTC, so the commission is unable to provide copies to consumers. Some states do keep franchise-offering circulars on file, and interested people can arrange to view them by contacting the state's finance, franchising, or business regulation department.

Canada has no federal agency regulating franchisors, although the Federal Competition Bureau is responsible for overseeing misleading advertising. The governments of Ontario, Alberta, and Prince Edward Island require companies franchising within those provinces to follow legislated requirements. Members of the Canadian Franchise Association (CFA) are required to provide a minimum level of disclosure, which is detailed in the "Disclosure Document Guide," available on the CFA website (www.cfa.ca) — click on "Already in Franchising," and then "CFA disclosure"). You can also find links to the applicable provincial legislation on that site.

How can I find out if there have been complaints against a company?

Unfortunately, there is no federal, state, provincial, or private organization in the United States or Canada that can confirm if a company is legitimate or not. The FTC or the Better Business Bureau can tell you whether a complaint has been filed against a company, but dishonest operators know this and often change the name and location of their organizations every few months to avoid detection.

The best way to protect yourself is to check the track record of a franchisor by talking to existing franchisees. The FTC recommends getting in touch with at least ten of them to make sure you get a clear picture of what is going on. In fact, the US Franchise Rule requires companies to give potential franchisees a list of the names, addresses, and telephone numbers of at least ten existing franchises in the same area. Try to visit a few of these locations to ensure they exist and that the contacts are not just ringers, who have been paid to give a glowing review of the franchisor.

You can request information about consumer complaints by writing to —

> Freedom of Information Act Request
> Office of General Counsel
> Federal Trade Commission
> 600 Pennsylvania Ave., NW
> Washington, DC 20580

Identify your letter as an "FOIA Request" and include your name, address, and daytime telephone number as well as the name and address of the company you are asking about. The FTC does not usually charge a fee for this service, but in case there are applicable costs, it is a good idea for you to indicate the maximum amount you are willing to pay.

You can also request information from the Better Business Bureau website (www.bbb.org).

How can I file a complaint against a company?

If you are having difficulty with a franchisor, you can send a written complaint to the FTC. This helps the commission identify companies and practices that may be illegal. You should describe your problem and explain what you think is misleading or deceptive in the company's promotional material, disclosure document, or offering circular. Mark each page "Privileged and Confidential" if you want the letter kept private. Include your name, address, and daytime telephone number and send copies (not originals) of any documents that support your case to the following address:

> Consumer Response Center
> Federal Trade Commission
> Room 130, 600 Pennsylvania Ave., NW
> Washington, DC 20580

The FTC also suggests individuals contact a lawyer to determine if there are any legal actions that might help resolve the problem.

How do I know what must be included in a disclosure document or offering circular?

The US Franchise Rule sets out what information a franchisor must disclose in an offering circular and provides a format for disclosure (go to the FTC website, www.ftc.gov, and click on "Legal Resources"). An alternative disclosure format, the Uniform Franchise Offering Circular (UFOC), is issued by the North American Securities Administrators Association and approved by the FTC. UFOC disclosure guidelines are available from the NASAA website (www.nasaa.org). Click on "Industry & Regulatory Resources" and then "Uniform Forms."

Current federal and state guidelines are contained in the *Business Franchise Guide*, published by Commerce Clearing House, that is available in most law libraries.

In Canada, since there is no federal organization that controls disclosure requirements, you're best to start with the Canadian Franchise Association's "Disclosure Document Guide," which is available on the CFA website (www.cfa.ca).

How can I find a lawyer who specializes in franchising?

The best way to find a lawyer who specializes in franchising is to check with your local state, provincial, or county bar association. Many of these organizations allow their members to identify specialties, which include franchise and distribution law.

In the United States, you can contact the American Bar Association for referrals. Go to the association's website (www.abanet.org) and click on "Find Legal Help."

In Canada, the Canadian Bar Association provides links to each of the provincial and territorial lawyer referral services. Check out the association's website (www.cba.org), click on "Public/Media," and then select "FAQ." The section "Finding/contacting a lawyer" contains a link to the referral service.

⊡　　⊡　　⊡

A franchise may be the answer for you, especially if you decide to get into a business you have no experience in. Just remember to do all your homework first. Go through any disclosure document with a fine-tooth comb. Get an accountant and a lawyer to review it as well. Visit as many existing franchises as you can. If you don't, you could end up losing thousands of dollars ... and your self-employment dream.

13

THE SELF-EMPLOYMENT PENSION PLAN

Let's sit back and think about retirement for a minute. In the old days you would look for a job with a good solid company, you'd work hard, the company would treat you well for 40 years, and you would retire with a nice pension, with health benefits thrown in for good measure.

CUSHY PENSION PLANS ARE DYING OUT

Many of those pensions were defined-benefit (DB) pension plans, which guaranteed a percentage of the average of your best years' salary (usually of the last three to five years) for life. The amounts were often even indexed to rise with inflation. With this type of plan, you didn't need to worry about how well the pension plan investments were doing from year to year. You were guaranteed an amount, and that's what you got.

What's happened lately? First of all, DB pension plans are going the way of the dodo bird. IBM was the latest company to announce it would be switching to a defined-contribution (DC) plan. With low interest rates and unpredictable stock-market returns, promising a certain pension to employees is just too great a risk for companies to assume. In a worst-case scenario, it could lead them to bankruptcy. You can't blame them for making the decision to limit their risk.

KEEPING A JOB IS GETTING TOUGHER

But forget about gold-plated DB pension plans. Many people don't stay with the same company for more than a few years these days, let alone long enough to receive a pension of any description. Here are some of the reasons it is getting tougher and tougher to keep a job:

- *Mergers and acquisitions.* Most mergers happen for one reason — it saves money. If two companies become one, there is going to be a lot of job duplication, especially in administration. Eliminating duplication is going to save the merged entity a lot of money … and it's going to cost a lot of jobs.

- *Competition from overseas.* There is no doubt that more and more cheap, quality labor is available in countries such as India and China. I've just read Thomas L. Friedman's *The World Is Flat: A Brief History of the Twenty-First Century* (Farrar, Straus and Giroux, 2005), which is a chilling warning that we ain't seen nothin' yet. It must be almost irresistible for a large corporation to ditch its North American workforce when it discovers it can hire five top-notch engineers in China for the price of one in New York.

- *Office politics.* No matter how good an employee you are, the longer you last in a company, the greater the chances that you'll wind up in conflict with someone and end up holding the short straw.

WHAT ARE YOU GOING TO DO?

As a small-business owner, you don't have the benefit of a cushy pension to fall back on when you retire. In all likelihood, you won't have a health plan either. You'll find it's hard enough to raise the kids and keep a roof over your head while trying to finance your business without pouring tens of thousands of dollars into retirement savings accounts.

So be it. But what are you going to do to make ends meet after you retire?

You're going to use the gifts that got you out of the rat race and into your own business in the first place — your skills, experience, knowledge, and drive.

FREEDOM 55?

I'm always mystified when I hear someone say they want to retire when they're 55. With the average North American now living to nearly 80 years, that means they will be spending about 25 years in retirement. That is a lot of time to fill, and will require a lot of money to finance.

But why do these people want to retire so early? Sadly, many of them hate their jobs. They are putting in "pensionable time" — in other words, suffering — until age 55 so they can enjoy the years after that. This does not make sense to me. For one thing, health concerns may leave them unable to enjoy retirement when it does come. Doesn't it make more sense to enjoy life while you are healthy?

The other question these early retirees need to answer is just what are they going to do with all their free time? In other words, what are their hobbies? Hobbies can be a real drain on cash (e.g., investing in expensive art, traveling the world) or more or less cash neutral (e.g., gardening, painting, volunteering for nonprofit organizations). The worst case is an early retiree with a superexpensive hobby. The money is likely to run out before his or her retirement years end.

There's another category of retiree besides the Freedom 55 type. I fit into this other category, and maybe you do too.

I LOVE WHAT I DO NOW — WHY STOP?

Most successful small-business owners love what they do. It's hard to put in all the effort necessary to keep a business going if you don't. I, for example, love what I do. Why would I want to stop doing it when I'm 55? I picture myself continuing to do at least some of what I currently do for a long time after age 55. In fact, I don't imagine I'll ever want to retire completely.

This takes a lot of pressure off me now because I won't have to sock away millions of dollars to fund my retirement. This can be the case for you too.

Your ability to continue working into your 60s and 70s will depend on the type of small business you set up. If you offer some type of manual labor, it's going to be more and more difficult for you to take on jobs yourself. If this is you, resolve now to grow the company enough so other people can do the physical work while you handle things like marketing and administration. Alternatively, set up a business that you'll be able to do yourself even when your body starts to slow down.

In my case, I write books and articles and give talks on financial matters. I'm also developing online learning modules and Web content for corporate, government, and educational clients. I can do this in front of a computer screen in the comfort of my own home, and I can continue doing it even when I'm starting to wear down physically. Of course I hope my mental faculties stay with me for a long time to come!

By the time I reach retirement age, I'll have a lot of experience attracting and servicing clients. I'll also have a large list of clients and acquaintances to draw upon. At that age my experience will be extremely valuable to the right clients. And value means good money.

At that point I'll be able to pick and choose. I will choose what types of jobs I like to do, and I'll be able to pick the clients I enjoy working for. I will do the work I like for people I like, and I'll only have to work as much as I want — two days a week? Three? Five hours a day? Ten hours?

Of course, people with full-time jobs can also decide to phase out of full-time work into part-time entrepreneurship, but they are less likely to have developed any entrepreneurial skills, including the ability to find and satisfy clients. They also won't have a client list from which they can choose only the best.

That is the beauty of the self-employment pension plan — the ability to keep busy and earn money doing what you love to do, even after you reach retirement age.

Forget Freedom 55. This is Freedom period.

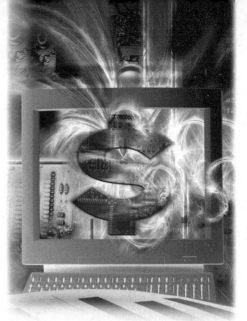

14

DO YOU STILL HAVE THE ENTREPRENEURIAL ITCH?

Okay, now you know that getting a small business of any kind up and running is almost never easy. You know that there will be hard work and long hours combined with the challenge of constantly attracting new clients or customers.

You realize there is risk involved. You could make sacrifices and put in long hours for months or even years and the business still may not make it.

On the other hand, you know your long hours and hard work may result in the dream: a business you love being involved in every day and that provides you with ample income to live the life you want, all without having to kowtow to an abusive boss or put up with coworkers who are a pain in the, well, you know what.

By reading this book, you've just taken the first step toward realizing your dream of starting your own business. I've tried to show you what it's like, warts and all. So do you still have the entrepreneurial itch? Do you still have that desperate desire to start out on your own?

Yes? Well then, go for it. Take the time now, before you get started, to research as many of the details as you can about what your business is going to do and how it's going to do it. If you haven't decided what you are going to sell or what services you are going to offer, start looking. Read newspapers, search the Web, visit the library. Ask people you know for their ideas and advice. Consider a franchise, especially if you are getting into a business you know little about. But beware: some business opportunities are bait from scam artists trying to steal your money and your dreams.

If you are in an industry that you love but in a job you don't, start watching how your company operates. How does it attract new customers and clients? How does it track the hours worked and how does it bill clients? If it's a retail store, how does the owner decide what inventory to buy and how to price it? Who are the best customers and where did they come from? How are employees treated? Is your employer always trying to find staff because no employee sticks around for long? Is there a better way to do things?

Once you've decided what it is your business will do, start working on finding clients and customers. Remember: start on a shoestring and keep your costs down. Start building the business in your spare time — before you quit your job.

Balance your life and your business. Don't let your business become your life. Remember that if you are married to your business and you're at it seven days a week, you won't have to worry about friends or family — they'll leave you and go somewhere else. Keep fit, exercise regularly, and go for medical checkups each year. It's impossible to operate a business from a hospital bed, so make sure you don't end up there.

Once your business is up and running, focus on improving it. Make sure you document the systems and procedures you use. Hire good people who are willing to listen and will treat customers, clients, and other employees with respect.

If you provide services, concentrate on billing what you and your employees are worth. Try to attract good clients, the ones who appreciate what you do for them and are willing to pay for it. A dream business has clients and customers who are great to deal with. If most of your clients are difficult, you may wish you had never started your business.

If possible, build a business that you can sell when you want to get out. Such a business must be able to operate when you are not there. Always be thinking: if I left for two months, would the business crash and burn? Make sure you get the advice of professional lawyers and accountants if you plan to sell. You are risking disaster if you don't.

Consider how your business ties into your retirement plans. Is it something you could continue to do in your 70s? Is it something you could continue to run and draw an income from, even if you're not doing the day-to-day work? If so, you will avoid the pressure to build up a huge retirement fund.

For me, every minute of every hour since I started my own business has been well worth it. I could never go back to a job working for someone else. I enjoy the work I choose to do. I can't think of anything I'd rather do.

How about you?

OTHER TITLES OF INTEREST FROM SELF-COUNSEL PRESS

Bookkeepers' Boot Camp: Get a Grip on Accounting Basics

Angie Mohr
ISBN 10: 1-55180-449-2
ISBN 13: 978-1-55180-449-1
$14.95 US / $19.95 CDN

Bookkeepers' Boot Camp teaches you how to sort through the masses of information and paperwork, how to record what is important for your business, and how to grow your business for success!

This book will show you the essentials of record keeping for a small business and why it's necessary to track information. It will give you a deeper understanding of your business and how it works.

Financing Your Business: Get a Grip on Finding the Money

Angie Mohr
ISBN 10: 1-55180-583-9
ISBN 13: 978-1-55180-583-2
$14.95 US / $19.95 CDN

Financing Your Business will show you, in an easy-to-understand manner, how to raise capital for your small business. Whether you are just starting a new business or you want to expand an existing business, this book help you to acquire the funds you will need.

Angie Mohr leads you step by step through the process and explores all the options available so that you can devise a financial plan that is suited to your company and goals.